PEACE

MARGARET PERRON

*Phillip~
May Peace
be with you
Margaret Perron*

HAZELDEN®

Hazelden
Center City, Minnesota 55012-0176
1-800-328-0094
1-612-257-1331 (FAX)
http://www.hazelden.org

Library of Congress Cataloging-in-Publication Data
Perron, Margaret, date.
    Peace / by Margaret Perron.
        p. cm.
    Final work in The Grace trilogy, of which the first work was titled Love and the second work was titled Grace.
        Includes bibliographical references.
        ISBN 1-56838-158-1
        1. Perron, Margaret, date. 2. Spiritual biography—United States.   I. Title.
    BL73.P47A3   1997
    973.72'092—dc21
    [B]   97—23172
                                                              CIP

Cover design by David Spohn
Illustrations by Randy Scholes
Text design by Nora Koch/Gravel Pit Publications

Editor's note
Hazelden offers a variety of information on chemical dependency and related areas. Our publications do not necessarily represent Hazelden's programs, nor do they officially speak for any Twelve Step organization.

Ten percent of the author proceeds from each sale of *The Grace Trilogy* will be donated to The Grace Foundation, an organization established in remembrance of Grace Zuri Love. The Grace Foundation has as its mission *Creating art and sacredness from the ordinary.*

For more information on The Grace Foundation, visit its web site at http://www.gracezurilovefoundation.com

Peace is dedicated to my husband, Donny Deeb, who brought peace to my life by becoming Father to my children; to Joe Perron, my earthly Father, who all my life told me, "Peace be with you"; to my heavenly Father, who all my life gave me Peace to be with me; and to Peace, who has always been with me.

And to you. Peace be with you.

CONTENTS

ACKNOWLEDGMENTS

In gratitude for Peace...

I want to say thank you to all those who were so considerate of the space I needed to leave unoccupied in order for this work to come to be. To all those I love who allowed me to be elsewhere so that this work could be completed. To all those who encouraged me and all those who believed in me, and especially to my family who supported me. And thanks to my Thursday-night dinner guests, Ed and Katie Deeb, who gave me the only excuse good enough to give up a night in front of my computer: that of pleasing my husband. And to my goddaughter, Alicia, who was a special gift in the final days of my editing.

In addition to the blanket thanks above to everyone in my family, I must mention my mother, who was just a little sensitive about some of the feelings I have revealed in *Love* and *Peace,* and who, despite that sensitivity, has been my champion every step of the way in this endeavor. Although the sometimes sad and confused thoughts I expressed when I spoke of her were true in a time and place that is past and gone, they didn't then, and don't now, obscure either the love she has for me or I for her. I hope my children, Ian, Mia, and Angela, know the same is true concerning them.

Thanks, too, to my spirit sisters, who have become such a large part of my peace, to my birth sister, Susan, and good friend Lou, whose companionship and words of wisdom were largely deleted from this book but not from my mind or heart, and to Ann Mulally Reilly, who always brought peace to my writing.

To each one of you I can only say that I have felt you start upon the road of Peace with me, I have felt you join me, and your companionship has sustained me through the quiet inward journey, bringing me back to you as surely as it has brought me back to myself and to God.

Thanks also to Dan Odegard for recognizing the value of *Peace,* for being affected by the Way of Peace, and for speaking of it to me in my own language: the language of words. No one says it more beautifully.

Much appreciation goes to Cathy Broberg, who realizes the power of words—both the keeping of them and the deleting of them.

If organizations have a soul, Hazelden's must be one of healing. My appreciation goes out, too, to Hazelden, the healing entity, for realizing the healing power of Peace.

And finally, thanks to Steve Lehman, my editor, who was willing to let *Peace* become part of him, who came to my table and said, "I cannot separate my emotions from this work," who gave me the gift of his tears and with those tears the reassurance that *Peace* was at the right place and in the right hands. In giving *Peace* to Steve, I received peace in return, the peace of knowing that he was the one who would bring *Peace* to the world in the way it was meant to be.

For all I am truly grateful.

INTRODUCTION

The spiritual experience is all about choice. How we choose to live our lives. How we choose to see ourselves. How we choose to relate to the world and the people around us. The spiritual experience seems, at first, to be about making many choices. But it is all about making one choice.

The spiritual experience is the choice—the decision—to do whatever is necessary to discover who we are so we can be who we are. I did not realize this was what it was all about when my journey began. But I had intimations.

I had reached a place where I felt my life was pretty

much in order: I had a religion I was happy with, Catholicism, and I had a sense that I could find what was missing in my life by bringing my religion and my life more together in some way—making my relationship with God more than just going to church on Sunday. So I began to pray in a way that was more personal to me than the way I had been taught—I began to pray by talking to God, in a journal format, on my computer. I also began to read books about spirituality. And I began to discuss what I was reading and thinking with two friends with whom I worked, Mary Love and Julieanne Carver.

Only a few months after opening a prayer file on my computer, I began a dialogue with an angel named Peace. This book recounts that dialogue.

What became immediately evident through this dialogue was that my life was not in the order I thought it was. Instinct took over as soon as I had this angel, this *authority,* to consult, and I did not ask weighty spiritual questions but the questions I really wanted answers to. It was only by Peace's tenacity and skill as a listener and as a guide that I learned anything at all. Because he saw into and through my questions to what was in my heart, and caused me to look there as well.

Hidden beneath each of my requests to Peace were some variations of the questions, Who am I? What am I to do with my life? and Why am I in pain? The answers, in their many forms, simply told me that the only one keeping me from being who I truly was was me. The only one who could free me from pain was myself. And that if I concentrated on freeing myself from pain and discovering who I truly was, the answer to what to do with my life would surely follow.

Peace always provided gentle and thorough answers. But he also always provided the only answer I was ready to hear. His responses to my questions became more sophisticated as my ability to hear became more sophisticated and as my willingness to learn grew. We think our willingness to learn is total until we confront our unwillingness to let go of old ideas. We think our desire to be guided is total until we confront our desire to have things the way we want them or the way we think they should be.

Perhaps Peace, himself, put it best when he said:

I can only guide you. Like a tour guide, I can proclaim the sights outside the bus window, the wonders that can be seen there, the paths that would be best to take and those that would be best to leave unexplored. But I cannot force you to look or to hear or to see more than you are ready for. Like the person on the bus, you see only the choices—so many things to look at, so many ways you could go. And like the person on the bus, you choose your own path—often knowing that it will be the one full of surprises, choosing the surprises instead of the sure thing.

Why?

To learn what you must learn in your own way. Because THIS IS KNOWN TO YOU. Despite your frequent requests for information and detail, YOU KNOW THAT YOU MUST FIND YOUR OWN WAY.

Does this mean that you will never choose to make your way the Way of Peace? It could mean this. But it does not have to. You do not have to continue to look about and see a thousand choices. You can, instead, look within and see one choice: the Way of Peace.

Choice.

It is more difficult than one would think to be asked— to be confronted with choosing to be more than what we are, more than what we have believed ourselves to be. I don't know why it is so much easier to choose to be *less,* but this is the way it was for me. I was willing to accept myself as flawed, guilty, and unworthy. I was willing to accept life as difficult, to see it as one struggle—one conflict—after another. But to be asked to see myself as perfect? To be asked to see life as joyous? These choices seemed impossible to make.

Choice.

Peace seemed, at first, to be asking me to look at reality and ignore what I saw there. Being asked to choose to trust in a distrustful world seemed like folly. Being asked to choose to open my heart seemed like an invitation for more hurt to come my way. But what Peace was really asking was for me to choose a new way of looking. To choose a new reality. I came to see that everything Peace asked of me was an invitation. An invitation to change my mind about myself and the world.

Having an angelic guide seemed, initially, to be the answer to my prayers. But soon, the reality of having a relationship with an angel began to pose its own difficulties. You do not just begin recounting angelic communication in day-to-day conversation. How does one say to one's husband, "I was talking to my angel the other day and he said . . ."? Peace thus became a call to choose what I believed in—a choice I believe we each must make, whether it be to believe in God or angels or ourselves or, preferably, all three.

Talking to Peace was also difficult in another way. It seemed to me that after talking with an angel, life should immediately change in some earth-shaking way. But it didn't. My life was still ordinary. I often went straight from talking to Peace on my computer to washing dishes or doing laundry or painting walls. But these things were not what I would have chosen to do had I seen a choice.

Choice.

There were days I would have given anything to be able to make Peace my life. Days when it seemed the dichotomy of talking to Peace and then going off to work was just too much. Had I been single, I truly think I would have sought a more religious life—say that of a nun. If I had been wealthy, I believe I would have chosen a reclusive life of quiet reflection and left the outside world alone for a while. I fantasized that there might be a grant of some kind that would fund me to stay home and talk to Peace and read books and discover what was sacred about life. But I didn't see any of these choices as real choices. I was part of a family and a household that needed two incomes. I was part of a family whose members' lives were not about to come to a halt so I could take a little vacation from life to seek the spiritual. Yet, it was never far from my mind that something miraculous was happening to me and that I was just going on with life as usual. It didn't seem right somehow. So Peace also became a call to extend the spiritual into my daily, ordinary life, to make Peace my life as much as I could within the confines of that ordinary life.

And I found that as I learned to apply the messages of Peace to my day-to-day life, my day-to-day life *did* change. Choices opened up to me where I had never seen them before. I saw that I could choose new ways of doing things, new ways of handling situations, new approaches to relationships. Little miracles seemed to be happening every day. My spiritual life began to *be* my life. My spiritual life began to *bless* my life.

Not that you'd always know it from these conversations. As I reviewed the Peace writing and found that it contained some of the most beautiful, spiritual, divine writing I had ever beheld, I couldn't believe that I could follow any of these passages with still another mundane question about another mundane detail of my life. I couldn't believe the patience Peace had with me. I couldn't believe how long it took me to "get" things. If you question from where this writing came, you might consider that if I were making it up, I wouldn't have made myself out to be so dim-witted. So *thick.* So unable to grasp the simplest truths. But as Peace would say, "how long" it took me to get something didn't matter in the slightest. The journey itself was just as important as the "getting there."

As I reviewed the Peace writing, I realized Peace and I rarely talked directly about God. Yet I always knew we were heading in His direction. I knew I was being prepared. I knew that even if my questions had not been about myself, my *self* was the starting point. We must start with ourselves because faith in ourselves is the hardest faith to find and until we find it, how can we have faith in anything else?

Perhaps the desire for life to change in some earth-shaking way is a desire to have an external "something" to place our faith in. It was hardest to believe in myself when I saw myself as the same woman I had always been, living the same life, doing the same dishes, scrubbing the same floors. But remaining the same *externally* forced me to look *internally* for change. Remaining the same externally caused me to see that while I might do the same mundane chores, I did them more peacefully. I came to live more peacefully because I became a more peaceful person—*inside*. I became a more peaceful person inside by learning to know my true self and by learning to let go of my false ideas about myself. I became a more peaceful person by choosing the way of Peace.

What is the way of Peace? A choice. A choice to see things differently. *A choice to find your own way.*

PEACE

Peace is a dialogue, an adventure, a journey, a discovery. Peace is an angel, a state of mind, a place of being. Peace is something felt and experienced and eventually known. Peace is an invitation. Peace is a beginning. Peace is a choice anyone can make.

I.

PRAYING

PRAYERS

March 19, 1995

I t is Lent. In church today, the mood was magnificent. Father Baz in his purple robes, the girls singing in choir. The mysterious sound of the prayers said in Aramaic. The wonderful language of the Mass. We pray to be humble, to be forgiven, to be blessed. We pray for our ancestors and for the departed, the living and the dead. We pray the Our Father together, Father with his eyes raised to heaven.

Today we heard the parable of the Prodigal Son. Father Baz said it was named incorrectly. The lesson comes from the father not the son. The father who waits to welcome his child with outstretched arms is like our Father.

There is so much love and community and family in religion. Even the ceremony and ritual of it. What family does not have its ceremony and ritual, a time for giving advice and a time for giving praise, and a time for giving and receiving forgiveness?

I am thankful to be part of this family. I am thankful to be able to ask for blessings on my children and my goals from a source greater than myself.

March 23, 1995

This whole process I am beginning—this preparation to buy a new home—has become a reassessment of my life. As I was clearing out some of the junk in my desk, I found, for instance, the paperwork related to my desire for a reverse tubal ligation. It reminded me of all I had hoped a new baby would bring to my family.

But I also found much concerning my struggles with the babies You were so good to give me. Everything related to my pregnancies and my children's infancy seems, in retrospect, to have been a struggle. It is one of the reasons I so desired a new baby. I wanted the chance to do everything right instead of everything wrong. I wanted, just once, to be wholly joyous about being pregnant from the moment of conception. I wanted, just once, to welcome a baby into a family and a home where love was not just a feeling but an environment. I loved Ian and Mia and Angela dearly. But I could too seldom provide them, when they were young, with an environment of love.

Thinking about all of this again has shown me that I do have that opportunity now, something my dear friend Mary will never have. Her loss of her daughter is a constant reminder of how lucky I am. A constant reminder of how grateful I should be.

I need Your help, Lord, in cherishing and providing for the children I have as I would a new child.

As I look forward to beginning a new phase of my life, a childless phase, as my children grow up and leave, I see that it is not they who are associated with the pain of the past but only me. In them I see only goodness. I feel only the joy they have brought, the fullness they have given my life. I know they will continue to do so. I pray there will be grandchildren someday when they are ready to bring new life into the world. But I realize how important the present is and how much of my life I have spent dwelling on the past and planning for the future. I need Your help, Lord, to remain rooted to the present.

There is so much I want to do. In my writing life alone there are a dozen projects I want to bring to fruition. I have no concept of which project is more important, of which You have put me on this earth to create. But I do feel that writing is part of my mission in life. And I thank You for this mission.

I guess the main thrust of today's prayer, Lord, is to help me live the life I would live (or have tried to live) had you given me a new baby. Give me the strength to cherish what I have as much as I sometimes long for what I don't have.

March 28, 1995

Sunday's sermon was about the paralytic and the miracle of Jesus. Father made much of the fact that Jesus did not just say, "Get up and walk," but, "Get up and walk. Your sins have been forgiven." Meaning that we are often paralyzed by our sins. He talked also about confession in this sermon—using the parallel of confession forgiving us for our sins and the miracle of the paralytic man to suggest that we can be healed not only in mind and soul but in body by confession—by seeking forgiveness.

I am more and more impressed by how my readings on spirituality so often mirror what is going on in Mass. I am comforted that my new spiritual teachers are Catholic. They draw often on their Catholic beliefs and especially on Catholic symbolism and ritual.

I thank God that I was raised in this wonderful tradition and that I have been given the opportunity to raise my children in this faith and in a loving environment—a community such as Holy Family.

I look forward especially, this Lent, to the symbolism of Lent and Easter, of the death and rebirth. As I feel myself being transformed—going from one phase of life to the next—this message is especially powerful to me and I know there is much I can learn from it, that it can teach me, this year.

March 29, 1995

I am stupidly envious of my friend Mary's spiritual experiences which have grown out of great sadness and pain. There is no great sadness and pain in my life right now—not even any great conflict. There is busyness, ambition, creativity, but nothing exceptionally good or bad. And in some ways, it is difficult. It is so new, perhaps.

It is difficult in that sometimes I cannot talk about my "things" because there is always someone with a greater need. But more than that, it is difficult on some psychological level not to be in the midst of something that is so personally moving. I, like Mary, have turned to spirituality in my quest to fill the role that pain and strife so often filled. I am not fool enough to want pain and strife back in my life. And my life is very full, but all in a normal sort of way. It is full of family and work and writing and planning to move, all but the writing being on a more physical than mental/spiritual/emotional level. And even the writing has not lately been writing on my book—the creative writing that fills me with my own personal bliss—but a form of writing convenient to the small amounts of time I have to spend on it.

So, the spiritual journey. I don't mean to portray it as second best, as "I don't have anything else going on in my life, so I am going on this spiritual journey." It has called me. It has captured my mind and my imagination. It has led the direction of my thoughts and my writing. And I guess I can only envy Mary if I don't see this as miracle enough for me. I have been envious because her journey is filled with a different kind of miracle.

I guess I had to write this to learn that that sort of journey is not my way. That this is the one appropriate for me. A journey in words. A journey of reading and writing and slow revelations.

And I may have had to write this to see the need to get back to my book. That, too, is a part of the spiritual journey I should not forget. Following my bliss is doing what God wants me to do and it is how I can bring myself closest to the divine.

Thank You for this gift and this miracle and for making me who I am. Help me to appreciate those things and use them to the best of my ability.

April 2, 1995

I want to say it's Easter because we celebrated Easter today as Mom and my brother Ray are leaving tomorrow for a trip to Georgia. Only goes to show how the ritual holy day and the celebration of it are linked in our minds.

First we went to Mass. My brother Michael arranged for the 10 A.M. Mass at St. Matt's to be said for Grandmother Ivie. It continues to give me a good feeling when prayers are offered for our ancestors, especially Grandmother Ivie, who was so tormented in life by mental illness. The time during the Mass when we remember our ancestors, the living and the deceased, is one of my favorite times. I list everyone in my head, from the grandparents right up to little Gracie Love. It is one of the only reasons I feel guilty when I miss church. The church rules don't bother me nearly so much as missing the chance to remember and pray for those I love.

I like Father Adrian, the pastor at St. Matt's. Today he talked about compassion. It was the sermon of the accused adulteress brought before Jesus. It was His famous "Let he who is without sin cast the first stone" line. Father commented on how the woman did not ask forgiveness and how Jesus didn't grant it.

The line I remember from the sermon is this: "Refuse to answer." Father Adrian talked of how Jesus refused to be baited by those who would follow law without compassion. He even used the Thomas Moore definition of compassion: *com* (with), *passion* (suffering). "Suffering with." "Putting oneself in another's shoes."

He talked about the recent murder of a young girl in the neighborhood, a girl whose grandmother was a parishioner. He used this story to illustrate how we cannot "fix" things. How we cannot make things better. We can only be there. Like Jesus. Be present. In compassion. An easy lesson to see in relation to a death, a more difficult one in relation to life. We have to refuse to "fix" things, he said. We have to refuse to give advice. What he suggests doing instead is asking how the situation has made the other person feel. Being there. Listening. Being compassionate. Things I hope I have done for Mary Love, things I have tried to do. Things I wish had been done for Grandmother. I couldn't help wonder how Grandmother's life would have been different if only she had had compassionate people around her. I pray that she is peaceful now. I can only believe my grandmothers must be angels in the afterlife, with little need of my prayers, with a desire only to be remembered, honored, and perhaps to comfort and guide.

April 8, 1995

I am reading, reading, reading, psychology and spirituality. Today reading one of the Emmanuel books, Emmanuel being an angel who speaks through a woman named Pat Rodegast. The messages of all the books are self-love, self-knowledge, self-acceptance.

I am also thinking about how difficult it is to do the right thing for your children. To love them is not always to be in accord with them, even if it is to always show your love for them, to accept and love them unconditionally. So what do you do about behavior you can't accept?

I see mainly the good in my children, and I believe that is as it should be, that is, their goodness is what *is.* They cannot be bad. They can only be misguided. I want to guide.

It is amazing how the spirituality I am reading about permeates everything. In my most casual encounters with people I hear messages from the readings (or from my own heart) to be kind, to be ethical, to let fate take its course.

Almost as relevant as my readings on spirituality was my annual birthday reading from the astrologer, Pat. I never really believed in astrology, but people I knew kept going to this astrologer and kept coming back with the most wonderful words. It was her way with words that attracted me to her, just as I am attracted to authors who weave incredible spells through the way in which they put words together. Pat's main message for me this year is about letting go, and it, too, is there in my readings. How you cannot willfully make things happen. That it is in letting go and accepting what *is* that you find release and freedom.

And it's all stirring around in me—random thoughts, not yet concrete—about how to live my life more fully. I already find myself breathing easier, being less stressed as I drive to work, being less rushed. Pat said this year would be like walking through water and it is beginning to seem that way. Even as I work and pack and write and fill my days as much as I ever did and more, there is a feeling of slowing down. Of letting go.

But I am still unsure of how to integrate this into the everyday world of raising children. I want to act in kindness and love; I guess I am being told in my soul, in my intuitiveness, to act with kindness and love, even toward the disciplining of my children, maybe especially toward my children. But I do not yet know practically how to use that kindness and love to instruct and guide. Will I be taken seriously if I act in kindness and love instead of in anger? And I can answer myself too, now that I've asked the question. Absolutely I can. But how do I get the point across about behavior that is unacceptable?

Lord, show me the way to make Your will my way.

PEACE

April 10, 1995

I think we've found our new home. Donny is excited about it, which means he will move on it. And there's a peacefulness about it that I like. There's a sunporch that will be mine all mine! For my office, for my meditation, for my reading room, for my soul!

Lord, if it is Your will and thus my will, let it work out.

April 17, 1995

I'm retyping my second mystery novel, *Who Killed the Mother?* into my Macintosh computer. I'm doing it for several reasons. One is to get it on a compatible, more up-to-date disk. One is that it is something I can do in between preparing for the move. One is to get it fresh in my mind again so I can finish it.

I just finished typing the scene where Mai, who is a fictionalized version of myself, has to deal, in a very public way, with her guilt over the way she raised her son. It's a catharsis of sorts, for her, and for me. To put it out there publicly, to *let it go.*

According to all my readings of late, our true selves are able to be revealed only when we surrender to truth and love. When we quit willing things to happen. When we accept what *is.* Our ISness.

A scary thought out of the Emmanuel books is that we are always ourselves—into the next world, into the next incarnation, into eternity. There are many starting overs but only one soul. Which is why we have to love ourselves.

Lent and Easter seasons were meaningful this year as they came at the same time that I have been reading so much about spirituality, the same time that I've been trying to let go, the same time that I've been trying to be more peaceful with myself, the same time I've been trying to let the rain fall and walk as if through water in my slowed-down physical life, while my soul life gallops along with its own power and speed, both slow and fast, both a rushing into the light and a retreat into the material world.

I had a truly divine experience on Holy Thursday. I went to Mass for the Washing of the Feet. My little nephews, Daniel and Tony, were among the boys who represented the twelve apostles and who had their feet symbolically washed by Father. That was why I went. To see them, to see the ritual reenacted. But I found, to my surprise, that the Blessed Sacrament was to be revealed and left out on the side altar. Parishioners were to stay with it, guarding it, being with it, in meditation and silence and prayer.

And I stayed. I wasn't planning to stay long. But tears started to stream from my eyes. I had to keep taking my glasses off to dab at my eyes. I felt lucky that the church wasn't full and that no one was looking at me. I couldn't understand why I was crying and I couldn't stop. It seemed as if every time I would think of leaving, the tears would start up again.

But I was not unhappy at all—I was overjoyed to have this wonderful opportunity to sit in this quiet holy place,

to have the church empty out, to have the light dimmed
and the music (classical) play from a tape player. I kept
thinking it was what church was supposed to be like and
never was. That a church should be a place for quiet meditation where the feeling of holiness could fill you. I can't
remember how many times I've wished that there were
more than thirty seconds given during the Mass for our
personal intentions. Time to talk to God. Father would
say, "Bow your head and pray for your intentions," and
you'd just get started and he'd be talking again. And I was
thinking about all of this, my eyes teary, my sight blurry,
when the candles burning beside the Blessed Sacrament
gave off a wonderful light. I'll never forget it. It was as if
all the flames of all the individual candles came together.
I even imagined, for a few moments, that the waves of
light came together in such a way that they formed a face
and that it was a sign to me. A sign that I was not alone,
that someone was with me. I could not quite convince
myself that it was just a trick of my eyes.

I stayed for hours.

Then there was Good Friday. It has always been, to me,
the most compelling religious day of the year. Even as a
child, I liked the mystery of it. The mystery of it drew me.
And still draws me. Maybe even more so now because of
this church of my husband's. Before marrying Donny, I
had never seen anything like it. The way the crucifixion is
dramatized. Jesus is taken off the cross and laid on a black
shroud. When parishioners enter the church, they bring

flowers and lay them beside the crucified Jesus. Later we all file up and kiss his feet. Then six men, like pallbearers, are called up. They raise Jesus over their heads and follow Father in a procession through the church. We follow to the sounds of a grief sung by Father, by the men, from the choir loft, but especially by the women that is so real it breaks your heart. The song is sung in Aramaic, the language of Jesus, but you do not have to know the words to know it is about the lament of Mary crying for her child, her *habeebee*. Because of my memory of this moving aspect of the service, I had invited Mary Love to attend.

I had turned the day into my first pilgrimage, something Pat had advised me to do, defining pilgrimage as a day I create for me, for my spirit, for my soul. I went to early Mass; went to one of my favorite places, the conservatory, to be among the flowers and the light; went to my favorite bookstore; brought the books with me to my favorite restaurant; went back to church. My daughter, my Angela, carried in baby's breath as a symbol of Mary's daughter, her Grace, and laid it on the crucifix. I carried flowers of my own. There was, once again, the Lebanese music, the chanting.

I wondered at my decision to invite Mary. This service always brought me to tears. It had the same effect on her but I could not do more than squeeze her hand, than whisper, "Are you okay?" She nodded. It was a sharing of grief. A primal, spiritual, ritual sharing of grief. I had never realized it so fully before. Then a burial. Jesus, in his bed of flowers, laid behind a stone.

Then Easter. The stone rolled back. The pain of death and grief followed by the joy of rebirth and celebration. Flowers handed out, the same flowers that had lain with Jesus. Eggs from the Maronite Youth Organization, watching my Mia give them to the other children of the church, to the old ladies. To old and young alike, a symbol of rebirth.

All of it happening together for a reason.

Easter Monday, back to church, a Mass said for Donny's grandma. His father, Ed, in and out of the hospital. The house we would like to buy still in limbo. My girlfriends at work into dreams and spirituality and the coming and going of Grace Zuri Love.

I sit, Easter Tuesday, and retype the passage of Mai's confession. Thirteen pages being typed as fast as my fingers can move, being moved by what I'd written.

Knowing this is the place of life and death and rebirth for me. Right here. In the words that somehow come out voluntarily here and nowhere else. In the forgiveness that happens here and nowhere else. In the fiction that is my way of examining my nonfiction. In my prayers. In my way of praying. In my way of synthesizing, with my heart and soul and not my mind, what has happened and is happening to me.

Here is where I let go. Here is where I am in my ISness. Here I am, the soul that will walk through eternity getting to know myself and accept myself and forgive myself.

Even the talk around the table at Easter with my husband's family . . . the gossip of babies born out of wedlock, and welfare moms and smokers . . . talk that goes into the heart of me and causes me to walk away with my humiliation fresh again.

But to come here and examine it. To have Lent and Easter. And to begin to let go.

April 24, 1995

I have entered a quieter time in my soul. It may be the passing of the holy season, it may be the passing of daily updates on otherworldly signs of Grace, it may be that I needed a quieter time. I am coming to believe that we are where we need to be.

And yet I keep reading. I picked up a novel again today, thinking it was time to get back to fiction, but it could not hold me. I went back to Thomas Moore, to *Soul Mates*, to read more about living the soulful life.

What amazes me is that I feel as if I have had the right idea all along. Part of the love affair I have with Thomas Moore is his ability to tell me that. To make me feel that I am on the right track. That before I knew anything about soulfulness, I was a soulful person. The giving of validity to those feelings can only help them to grow. For that I am thankful.

I am also continually astonished by the connectedness of everything I have been reading. It is as if all the things I've needed to hear are suddenly available to me. How can I help but be thankful?

PEACE

Besides reading Thomas Moore, I have been reading the
Emmanuel books. When I first heard of them I thought
they were sex books! Not so. But they are books written
by an angel, so in their own way just as embarrassing—or
almost as embarrassing (at least around certain people)—
to be reading. Yet Emmanuel's message is incredibly
soothing and forgiving. *ISness* is an Emmanuel term, as is
oneness. All things are one in love is what this basically
means.

His teachings are the same as those of Jesus: Love thy
neighbor as you love yourself. Yet he goes into the more
complicated aspect of loving self more than I have known
of Jesus to have done, perhaps because it is more what we
need now. He talks about how we can have made no mistakes because everything has a reason, a divine reason.
How releasing that is! He talks of fear and guilt as the ulti-
mate in destructive forces and urges us to let go of them.
He preaches love and kindness, which is very literally the
same as Moore's discourse on soulfulness and manners.
Both speak to the integrity of the individual. Both talk
about a kind of surrender and letting go of willfulness,
bringing me full circle to my theme for the year of *letting
go.* And interestingly, Emmanuel talks about our forget-
fulness and urges us to let memory come back to us.
Memory of other lives, memory of our divinity.

These readings have imbued in me the consciousness
to slow down and *breathe*, to quit rushing. To take my time

and smell the first hint of rain on the spring air. To be kinder to people. To look at others, even—and maybe especially—those I see on the street, and think, *There goes an angel.* The readings are reminders. Perhaps this is what Emmanuel means when he urges us to *remember.* A remembering that he and Moore both speak of when urging us to be present in the moment.

Finally, Emmanuel says visualize what you want and you can make it happen. Last night I began visualizing a publisher just finishing my book and calling my agent, Dan O., who will then call me. It did not happen today. It may happen tomorrow. Pat thought by the 27th, which is Thursday. Wouldn't that be something! But what did happen today was a call about the home Donny and I want. We missed the call, yet it has occurred to me that although I did not get the phone call I consciously asked for, perhaps I got the one I needed. We shall see.

April 28, 1995

The fated April 27 has come and gone. In the afternoon, I received a letter from Dan O. Its very appearance signaled to me that it was not going to be good news. Good news would have come by phone. Nothing in me expected the news I got, however: that Dan has taken a job with Hazelden Publishing and is leaving the agenting profession. It was a cruel irony coming on that fated day. *What does it mean?* I ask myself. *Why did it happen?*

Why do we even ask such things? Is it the mind trying

to explain the unexplainable? the unknowable that only God knows? Or do we all "know" our life plan, as Emmanuel suggests, but have just forgotten it?

I suppose "why" is a way we lead ourselves into feeling better or worse instead of just accepting or feeling the "now," the "present tense" of what has happened. If we can give some historical reason, we explain it for our mind even if our heart doesn't understand it any better. I can conjecture that it was meant to be because I was meant to find a better agent or because I was meant to concentrate on the house right now, but I would only be guessing.

For now I have chosen to believe that this ending is not definitive, that when Dan follows up on the manuscripts he has sent to publishers before ending his contractual arrangement with his authors, mine will be accepted. Until I am sure that that will not be so, I can put the matter of how I feel about it—the "whys"—aside. I can be in the flow a little while longer, letting my faith in Dan and in my writing be my guide.

April 29, 1995

The girls are in Chicago and Donny and I are alone, as we will be often the rest of our lives. We had a very nice, very sexy evening, and in the middle of it I found myself feeling very happy and realizing that Donny and I both had chosen to be happy—that there had been many instances, when we could have chosen to be miserable, irritable, finding our passion through dissent rather than happiness. And I know that we consciously chose happiness, just as I can see that some people have chosen unhappiness. For many, of course, there are temporary phases of unhappiness with divorce or other problems, but I can definitely see that some have chosen unhappiness as a way of life. Thank You, Lord, for helping Donny and me choose happiness. Please help my family and friends choose happiness too.

It also occurred to me last night that if I must find a reason for Dan O.'s flight from agenting that is personal to me, it may be that I needed to be centered in home and family in order to realize and appreciate the happiness I have—including the purchase of our new home, which today became a reality. I may have needed to understand that my home, family, and especially my marriage is as important as my writing. And I can see that I may not have fully realized this had I received word that I would be published, and had my thoughts centered mainly on myself and my creative life. So, thank You, Lord, for my blessings, in whatever form they come.

THE IN BETWEEN

May 1, 1995

Have I mentioned that the girls are in Chicago? I was apprehensive before they left. It seemed to me that it was going to be some kind of a test. How was I going to handle it when my girls were gone (for good)? What was it going to be like living in a household of two? What would it mean for my marriage? How would it feel?

I now admit the anxiety was stronger before the girls left than it is now. I have always been one for anticipation, for both the best and worst of what life has to offer. Some of the things I discovered were good sex, pretty good talk, and good eating with Donny. It was nice not to worry about having to fix meals for anyone but ourselves. It was nice not to have the phone ringing or tied up. It was nice to have rooms stay the way I left them, to have only myself to blame if I couldn't find my comb. In short, the girls physical presence was not missed and I learned valuable things about what life will be like when they're gone, that is, that I'll probably like it. This seems significant because it has scared me—as if there will be this horrible void when they are gone.

What I do miss is their love and their personalities, their spirit, their souls. I had a wonderful conversation with Angela before she left. She was talking about her memories in this house. One was how her window always rattles. Another was coming in from outside on a winter day with the smell of snow still lingering. Sound and smell. It made me realize how soulful she is. And when I have such thoughts, I feel as if I'm being a little disloyal to Mia, who I know is soulful too, but who has a harder time expressing herself.

I have never doubted my son's soulfulness, although it has been a constant flirt with the shadow side of things. I know Ian is a tremendously "feeling" individual and much like me. While he literally ran away from things he did not know how to deal with as he was growing up, I ran away also, but to an internal world. You would think, understanding this, that I would be able to help him more, and yet I have always felt helpless to assist him. His running away seemed merely to bring my powerlessness with him to the surface. There was no longer even an illusion then that I could parent him. And it seemed almost that this was why he ran. To show that Donny and I had no control—that I had given up my right long ago and that Donny, as a stepparent, had never had any. In the absence of a consistent father figure, Ian had filled in as man of the house for too long to ever accept parenting again.

Mia, too, I think, is more like me than Angela is. Angela, as young as she is, is the most accepting of who she is and the most ready to let things come to her. She is less wounded by life, I think.

Mia hides her soulfulness with an outward display of fun-lovingness. Ian hides his with his dark side—the side where all his passion now (still) lurks. I hope, I pray, Ian will find a passion for the bright side as well. And Mia, I hope, I pray, will find a way to channel her energies into soulfulness. She, I think, is least familiar with herself and so, in a way, has the most growing to do. At the same time, however, I think she is the one of my children best equipped for daily life. She works hard, plays hard, and doesn't spend too much time trying to figure things out like the rest of us do.

It is now 2:20 P.M., Donny has gone to work, and I am alone. I had looked forward to being alone this weekend. To me, there is something almost divine about alone time, and with the girls actually out of town, the alone time took on even more of an appeal. Friday, Donny was supposed to work until 6:30 P.M. He didn't. I left work at 2:00, saw the girls off on their bus, came home, and he was here. So I painted the garage.

All weekend we worked very companionably together, the roofers were here putting on the roof, people were in and out constantly.

This morning Donny's boss called and said he didn't have anything for him except some couple-hour-long job. So he stayed home and pulled down the ceilings upstairs until twenty minutes ago.

I am, at last, alone for a few hours but I'm in the middle of painting the hallways. And yet, it's no big deal. There was a time, not long ago at all, that planning a four-day, alone-time weekend and ending up with less than four hours alone and having to work during part of them would have driven me wild, made me really frustrated and angry.

So, I think, I'm growing up, not having tantrums when things don't go the way I had planned. Besides, I've had enough small doses of alone time that I'm not in desperate need of it; I've got a house to sell and the reality is I have to work; and anyway, I enjoyed being with my husband.

One of the things I like about being alone, even if I'm working, is setting my own pace. I work a little, have a cigarette break, work, have a reading or writing break, etc. I'm getting more comfortable with setting my own rhythm, even when Donny's around, but I'm always aware of how much time I'm taking and what he's doing, and wondering if he'll think I'm loafing or whatever. I also get to listen to my classical music when I'm alone, which is also a treat, and smoke wherever I want, which is also a treat. This is my first break.

I've been reading recently that it may be possible for people to talk with their angels and I think on my next break I'll attempt that. There's been a feeling in me, ever since Holy Thursday, that something "more" is awaiting me, somehow. All these wonderful, miraculous things have been happening with my friends at work. Mary has actually received messages of a sort through her computer. Julie heard a divine Voice and has been having these epic, detailed dreams that often connect her to Mary. It may only be wishful thinking, but it makes me feel as if something miraculous awaits me too.

Dearest Angel,

I think I have felt you with me since my earliest child-hood, certainly in my most tormented times when you would tell me I was special and a part of me believed you. Thank you. That voice that said I was special kept me living as much as I could live. Feeling as much as I could feel. There has always been a wonder in me, something that embraced mystery. It is this part of me that is willing to believe I can talk to you. It is this part of me that says it makes sense. Will you talk to me?

THE IN BETWEEN

Smell the sweetness. You are sweet. Don't try to force it, to will it, just let it come. It is there in the in between, between thought and feeling. Breathe. Feel your heart.

Why does it feel so heavy? As if it will break?

It's trying to open. To let joy in.

Is that my next lesson?

Yes.

Thank you. What shall I call you?

Peace.

Thank you. You are there in the in between?

Yes. Like white. Like space.

Space between the letters and words?

Like space. Like smoke.

Is it okay that I smoke?

Everything you do is okay.

Really?

If you give thanks for it.

Count my blessings?

No. You are blessed. What you do is blessed. No counting. Look in between.

In between the numbers there are no numbers?

Something like that. You're getting it.

Will you help me with my writing?

I am always helping you.

I want to know if my writing will be recognized. I'm sorry it seems so important to me but it is.

Look in between. This time is in between. Time is in between. Don't worry about time.

Will you help me do that?

Of course I will.

Do you mean that in time I will be recognized, but that there is not time? That's hard to understand.

Everything is. Don't worry about time. This is a very important message. Relax. Smell the sweetness.

I never realized how often time comes up. I was just going to ask, Do you mean smell the sweetness of this time?

Forget time. When it is important that you not be disturbed, you won't be.

Thank you. I like your name.

You gave it to me. It has always been my name. Dearest. Remember to rest.

I left my computer screen just the way it was and went off

to paint some more. It seemed almost goofy to leave an angelic communication to go paint but I could not let the brushes and rollers sit too long, and I felt a need to have accomplished a certain amount by the time Donny got home. I also didn't know what else to do. If I hadn't had the painting to do, what would I have done? What did one do after one talked to an angel? I hadn't thought that far ahead. I hadn't thought what it would mean. I hadn't thought to ask certain questions. It had been an impulsive act. Now I wasn't certain how I felt about it. But it seemed as if, as I painted, I kept getting messages. I didn't feel alone the way I always had. Someone else was in my mind, in my thoughts. I spent about an hour painting and then went back to the computer:

I was just going to come back and say thank you, Peace, for talking to me, but since I left here, you have been with me and I have received a couple of very clear messages:
1. Listen to my sister. Really listen. Not just to what she has to say about me but to everything she has to say.
2. That my painting is just as important as anything else I'm doing today, which also means, I would think, that whatever I am doing at the moment is what is important, but also,
3. That it's important to leave this house better than we found it. To leave it with love, in good shape, well taken care of. Because it's going to be important to the people who buy it. I almost have a feeling that the people who

buy it might end up being our friends. But perhaps it is the feeling that all people are friends whom I should do my best for.

Peace, has that heaviness in my heart always been joy waiting to come in?

Yes.

I'm already really hearing what you said. I'm sitting here reviewing what has happened, worried about the time and that Donny will come home and find me taking a break when I'm not as far along as I should be. Why have I set him up to be such a censor? All I'm doing is cheating myself out of these minutes (time again) when I could be enjoying my aloneness. Thank you for making me aware of this. I'm thinking that you have something else to say that has drawn me back here. Here I am, wanting to wrap up and summarize, and you are still there to talk to me. This is also a lesson, I believe. To quit wrapping up and summarizing prematurely. Was that your message or is there something else you would like to tell me?

It's in between. [The cursor is flashing erratically]

In between what?

Don't will it. Let it come. You're doing great.

In the spaces in between breathing in and out? Is that where you are?

I am inside. In the blood flowing through your veins.

I keep willing it and I keep thinking about time. And this makes me wonder if I need meditation exercises or if this is an okay means of communication as it is.

Both. Relax.

I am feeling that there is some symbolism for me in the letter *X*.

Good. It is in between yet connected. Study it.

It is two lines going off in different and opposite directions. It is two *V*s one right-side up and one upside down. It is a cross. It is like the shape of an hourglass.

Good. What else?

It is in the word relax. *Lax* is associated with laziness, something I fear being.

Leave fear behind.

Help me. I'll try.

Trying is all that matters. Go back to painting now. There is something about white *also.*

I realized several things while I painted. The first came to me almost immediately: *White* is in between, neither here nor there, not a color but not not. It is the color of Peace, I think. Next, I realized what I was doing with the white paint: I was covering over the bad spots, erasing them, so to speak. Along with that thought came the "white" of baptism, holy communion, in short, sacrament, purity. Then I thought of painting over in white as being a fresh start, a blank page, a new beginning. I made my series of Xs on the wall, something my sister, Susan, had taught me to do, and her words about how to paint came back to me: "Make an X and then fill it in and you don't miss anything." Sounds kind of profound now.

X is the number ten in Roman numerals. The number ten in numerology is a transition number between the roots and the compounds—an in between number.

And as I filled my Xs in, I realized that the Vs it makes are not only right-side up and upside down but crosswise. Four Vs each reaching out into infinity.

Now I do feel it is time to sum up. From my first conversation with my angel I learned its name: Peace. I learned of a symbolic color that represents him: white. I learned what my symbol of our connection will be: the X—and I have seen a lot of symbolism which I can spend some time thinking about. Wow!

Thank you, Peace.

You're welcome.

Now—am I sure I'm talking to an angel? Yes. Maybe one that is part of me, in the sense of all things being one. I guess I could say I'm talking to myself, and it is a little like that. But I did get tears in my eyes and feel them fall down my cheeks when I was told my lesson now is to learn joy. I didn't feel finished until I was finished. I did feel what I wrote about—the heaviness of my heart. Is it gone? No. Is it there all the time? No. It wasn't before either. But it is occasionally. When your heart is heavy, you know it. I know I wasn't thinking of *peace* or *white* or X before I sat down. I had been reading about angels and was hoping some name from the readings, like Uriel, wouldn't pop up. They didn't. Peace did. It may seem more of an expression of a feeling than a name but that's fine with me and fine with Peace, apparently. The X was something Susan had said in relation to painting, no reason for my conscious mind to bring it up in relation to an angel. So all in all—yes—I think I was talking to my angel. Amen.

I looked up X in my *Webster's* dictionary:

> the twenty-fourth letter of the English alphabet
> to indicate one's choice or answer by marking with an X
> an unknown quantity
> a mark shaped like an X used to represent a signature of a person who cannot write
> to mark a particular point on a map
> a symbol for a kiss in letters
> the Roman numeral 10
> a person or thing unknown or unrevealed

an abbreviation for extra
an abbreviation for Christ
the power of magnification (in optical
instruments)
x-ed: to cancel or obliterate, usually with a series
of *X*s

Dearest Peace,   May 2, 1995

Since I talked to you, I have been censoring myself. I think of a question I want to ask you, but then I think that I already know the answer to it (as in, Was that you with me in church on Holy Thursday?) or that the question is superfluous and I don't need the answer. Yet I don't want my conscious mind to mislead me. And time is still almost impossible for me to release. And finally, I think I should be satisfied with what I got yesterday, that to expect you to speak to me twice in two days would be expecting too much. Yet I know I am censoring and shouldn't be. The heaviness is back in my heart. Are you with me?

I'm always with you.

I don't want to ask questions then. I just want you to talk with me. What do I need to hear?

The music. What is there right now. Smell the sweetness. Close your eyes.

I am being too willful.

Quit censoring yourself. Love yourself.

Is there something else the painting has to teach me? Do we need to talk about the research I've done? The *X* seems particularly meaningful.

It is. It is multiplication, duplication, more than one.

Meaning I am more than one?

Meaning I am with you and more, much more. An infinity. Center. Go to the heart of yourself. X marks the spot.

My heart.

Your spirit, your divineness. Your in between.

In between being where you are. Between the physical and the divine.

I am the physical and the divine. It is all there. Within. Go within.

I am too into my mind right now. This feels stilted. I'm not sure you're talking to me.

Go paint.

Later—

I painted and now I'm taking a break. Here's what happened while I painted.

After just a few minutes, I realized that I wanted to listen to the Moody Blues. At once I knew that the Moody Blues were perfect: celestial music, vocals, and words. Every song spoke of a spiritual quest, I'm sure of it. Soon

I was singing along while I painted the hallway going up the stairs (relevant? ascending?). Then "Tuesday Afternoon" came on and it made me smile because it actually was *Tuesday afternoon*. While I was singing along with the song, another voice, another breath, came into me. My voice echoed and filled the stairwell. At first it scared me, and I coughed, almost as if there was too much breath in me. Then I sang out again and when I realized it was still there—this other voice—I opened my mouth wider to let it all come out.

Later—

I'm back, Peace.

Another Moody Blues song, "I'm Just a Singer (In a Rock and Roll Band)," came on after I had heard song after song that spoke to me with such clarity about the desire for a spiritual life. And I found myself thinking, *No. They're not just singers in a rock and roll band.* I thought, *They're messengers of the angels.*

Right.

And I wondered if there was a double message for me. A message in a message.

In between.

Yes. Is the message about me and my writing or is it just my hopes that want to make it so? Every time I ask a question about my writing, I'm afraid of the answer and I think I block it.

I am with you, writing or painting.

You're going to have to be clearer with me about the writing. Please.

I am also with you when you are blocking. Relax and the answer will come to you. This computer isn't the only way we communicate. Don't strive so to make the answers come in this format. Listen and you will hear.

But I did hear. I heard that song title "I'm Just a Singer (In a Rock and Roll Band)," and heard how limiting it was. And I thought, *I am just a writer* and thought it was the same.

You're right.

So I am also a messenger?

Of course you are.

And so my message will be delivered?

Of course it will.

When? Can I ask how soon?

Forget time.

I'll try. But this has greater import for my coming books doesn't it?

You are growing aren't you? Your growth will be reflected. You don't have to get it all at once. Relax. You don't have to go it alone.

45

Will you help me see the way in book number two?

I am helping you. It's there inside you waiting to come out.

Let go. Let God?

Relax.

I'm not sure I know how.

I'm not sure, either. Learn how.

May 4, 1995

Today is Thursday, the last and fourth day of what was going to be a three-day "work on the house" vacation. Everything takes longer than I think it will and I am finishing up work in the kitchen. First, however, I needed to get my car tabs, and then I wanted to go to church as I usually go when I'm off work.

While I was driving, the morning wisdom came to me. What I clearly realized is how afraid I have been about the book I've been working on. I can barely get the words out to ask for blessings on it, can barely pray for its success. The words always seem to get stuck. And then there was my older notion that I could only pray for a limited number of things, and I must always pray for the health and happiness of my family first. So out of that, I came up with calling the book my offspring so I could include it in my prayers for all my offspring. Now I have realized that I don't have to limit my prayers, and still it was hard for me to ask for my book. This morning I discovered why.

Fear.

In the Emmanuel books especially, fear is talked about as the greatest enemy. As I read this, I found myself thinking that I don't fear that much. I don't live in fear. I am not afraid to walk out on the street at night, not afraid of death, and so on. Then as Emmanuel talked more about fear, I realized he was also talking about things like fear of humiliation, fear of failure. Still, I didn't think it was a big problem for me.

And yet, I have known for some time that I am fearful concerning the book. All I had to do was think about calling an agent and I was seized with fear. All I had to do was attempt to write a book proposal or letter concerning the book to know—to be overcome by—fear. In a way, I thought this was good. The fear felt a little like excitement, and I thought there should be those things we care so much about that we get fearful and excited about them. Excited, maybe. Fearful, no.

So when this occurred to me, I tried to examine where the fear came from. There is some fear of failure, fear of humiliation, but the main cause of the fear, I think, came from feelings of unworthiness. *Who am I to think I can be a published author?*

This wasn't real conscious stuff. Consciously, I could tell myself I worked hard, but even now, as I try to finish the sentence, it catches a little: I worked hard and I deserve to be rewarded for my labors. I deserve recognition. And just at this instant it is occurring to me that recognition may be the other scary stuff. *Recognized* implies being known. Fame does not scare me, but being known is a little scary. Letting anyone read my book is scary because it is so much me—it is like inviting them to know me. And is how can I invite the world at large to know me if I am not worthy? I know some people would read the book and think it is autobiographical and think what a poor mother I am/was—but that isn't the worst of it. The worst of it is what I think. I need to get to the place where I do not have to defend myself or my work because I am at peace with myself/my work. PEACE.

So beginning today, thanks to my angel, I am letting go of my fear. I am saying out loud: "I have worked hard and I deserve to be published. I am letting go of my fear regarding my writing. I am worthy to become a published author."

The other thing that was incredibly apparent this morning is my need to become peaceful with doing what I am doing when I am doing it without worrying about time. I am also worthy of my breaks.

Dearest Peace,

I have come to many realizations since our talk. And I have many things to work on. Thank you for pointing those things out to me. And thank you for steering me to the Moody Blues. I've listened to them all day and could go on listening to them.

I also told my "spirit sisters," Mary and Julie, about you.

I am so honored that they want to come over tomorrow and share with me what has happened. Yet it worries me a little bit. I don't—

Want to seem special. You are.

Thank you. I also don't want to minimize the experience or make it grander than it was. And there is some fear (sorry about that) about it. I'm not sure what it is.

There is nothing wrong with you. You are getting my messages. What more is it you want?

Can I see you?

I am there in the in between. Like a reflection, a shadow, a flower, a flame.

Like the wick of a candle or stem of a match with a golden glow on both sides?

Yes. And like the smoke that rises from it and like the sky.

ON THE THRESHOLD

Dear Peace,   May 5, 1995
     Julie and Mary just left. Thank you so much,
Lord, for giving me friends to share this experience of Peace with. Peace, I am sure you were there with
us as we talked about you. As Julie said at one point, the
whole group of you—all of our angels—were probably
getting a laugh out of us. I like that image.

So do I. It was quite accurate.

I've been listening to more Moody Blues. The CD title is *On
the Threshold of a Dream.* Is this a message?

Threshold *is an accurate description of this place.*

Yours or mine?

Both.

Am I on the right track, giving up my fear about writing?

You are always on the right track.

I have a feeling releasing that fear is the first step in my journey as a writer.

As a messenger.

This is a beginning for me then, isn't it? I've found you and the path is getting clearer.

That's what I'm here for. To clear the path. To clear your fear. To clear your mind. To open your heart to joy.

I have a hard time remembering joy. I know I'll need help experiencing it.

You'll have help. But you must let go and open your heart in order to experience it. You're still blocking. Your skepticism is okay. Fear must go.

Am I fearful of opening my heart as well as fearful of time and of sending my writing into the world?

You know you are. All those lessons you learned when you were talking to your diary as a young girl closed your heart. It has been closed a long time. Your family has been trying to open it. Listen to them. Let them in. They will not hurt you.

Another fear—fear of being hurt.

It is the same fear as all the others. Fear is pervasive in you. It has you locked up tight. It makes you unrecognizable to other angels who could help you. Your light is blocked. It all has to do with opening your heart. I promise you will not be hurt if you do this—when you do this.

It's a process isn't it? Not something I can do in one day?

If you choose to make it a process, it will be a process. If you choose to do it in one day, it will be done.

Fear is making me want to make a process of it, isn't it?

Let go of fear. Breathe. Smell the sweetness. Open to it.

My friends were so sweet today. Yet I do feel slightly removed from them, from everyone—the closed heart?

The closed heart.

What is a beneficial way for me to see you?

Only you know that. I will be as you choose me to be and who I am. You cannot change me or my love for you. I will always be with you. There are others for whom this is true also. Nothing you can do can make them not love you. You see, it is safe to open your heart.

Just what I want to be I'll be in the end?

Exactly. If you want an open heart, you will have an open heart.

I want an open heart.

No qualifications?

No. I am ready to be recognized.

Then I am very happy.

I can feel that.

Trust what you feel. Nothing you think or write is wrong, or not from me. You are from me, I am from you, we are one.

Thank you. I needed that permission to accept what comes out here as the truth.

There won't be any lies here. I assure you of that.

Thank you. Thank you. Thank you. I am truly grateful. I love you.

Then you love yourself.

Love has made me uncomfortable, even in the songs. I need to accept love too, don't I?

That is the most important thing. The most important. Self-love. Self-love will get rid of the censor for you, the time demon, the fear.

Is there a shedding I need to do?

Only of your fear and your closed heart.

The Moody Blues' lyrics still go through my mind, lyrics about stepping to the other side of life. Is that what I've been doing with these conversations? Stepping to the other side?

To the in between. To the threshold. To the precipice. Once there you must make a leap of faith.

Isn't that what this is? A leap of faith? Believing that I am talking with an angel named Peace?

That has taken you to the threshold. Now you must leap.

How? Figuratively? Literally?

In your heart.

Leap in my heart. I don't know how to do that.

Yes you do. Let your heart rise up. Let it be your voice. Let it leap from you.

By opening my heart?

By opening your heart.

I said I want to open my heart. What else must I do to make it so?

Open it. Imagine a door that keeps feelings in and keeps love out. Here is the key. I am handing it to you. You see, the light was just seeping out the cracks before. Now it is brilliant. You didn't need to be afraid to open it.

Now what?

Now prop it open. Here is a brick, as heavy as your heart used to be. That's right. You can keep the brick for a while until you learn to keep it open on your own. See, no process when you let go of fear. You replace process with action. It's done. There's no going back. I'll be the keeper of the brick. You aren't to worry about it. When you're ready, I'll remove it. Meanwhile your heart is open. Everything happens for a reason. Remember that, dearest. And remember to rest.

One more quick thing. I know you are there in my dreams. And more. How can I remember my dreams?

With your open heart. They will flow in and out of your heart. Pay attention to your heart when you awaken. Listen to your heart. Listening is very important right now. You don't have to listen for that door to your heart slamming shut. Remember, I am the keeper of the brick. It is open for good. The dreams will cross this threshold of your open door where you will have access to them.

Thank you so, so much. I will carry my open heart with me as I work today and as I interact with others today and get used to how it feels. Thank you, Peace.

You're welcome.

Dearest Peace   May 7, 1995

Please remember how literal I am (which I didn't even realize before now) and give me clues or aides to help me be less literal—or I guess you probably already are, because I got it. I got, from your mention of my diary-keeping days, a true message about the time when I closed my heart.

I had such good parents, Peace, such a good family. I've never understood why I turned out so bad or why I felt so hopeless so young. Truly, by the time I was fourteen, I was so certain I was unlovable. Oh sure, my mom yelled at me a lot, but I deserved to be yelled at. She had a hell of a time with me, Peace, a hell of a time. I'm sure she didn't understand any more than I did what was wrong with me or why I couldn't make it right. It seems, looking back, that all I wanted was for someone to love me. How could I have thought my family didn't? Why did I turn to boys? And when I did, why couldn't I have found one good one instead of a string of jerks, each one making me feel progressively worse about myself?

Were you bad, Margaret, when you were fourteen years old? Can you honestly tell me you were bad then or that you are bad now?

No. That's not what I meant exactly. When I said I turned out bad, I just meant I was not good. Not a good student, not a good daughter.

Margaret, were you bad when you were fourteen?

No, Peace. I was sad. But I was not bad. I was not what people expected me to be. I was not what I expected me to be. I was a disappointment. But I was not bad.

Thank you, dear Margaret, for finally seeing this. It was only your feeling that you were bad, dear one, that brought to you people who did not treat you as if you were good. You were a neon sign announcing: "Here I am, someone who does not deserve to be treated well." It was as if you advertised and they came. You think that your thoughts and feelings about yourself are private, that they don't send out neon lights. You are wrong. Watch, dear one, as your thoughts about yourself change, how those around you change, how they treat you differently.

I thought my inner thoughts had changed a lot since I

was thirteen, since my diary-keeping days. I hope they have. But at least I "got it" Peace, got what you were referring to. And I got the *threshold* too, which is a very clear description to me—both symbolic, as in the open door to my heart, and literal, as in the meaning: a beginning, the outset, a point at which physiological and psychological effects begin to be produced. Wow!

Which leads me to this morning, Monday morning, when I should be at work. I called in with a lie about getting estimates, which I guess is okay but it would have been better had I told the truth. But the truth is that Donny has gone out of town to work at someone's cabin, the girls are in school, and I felt as if I couldn't waste this alone time, this time when I knew I would not be disturbed.

All of which is well and good except that I began immediately wasting the morning by feeling guilty about it and by continuing to fear that I will be disturbed. So now I am trying very hard to be in the Now. I just finished *Emmanuel II* last night and the whole final section was about being in the Now and how it is the most important thing. I am trying to believe that what I am doing now is what I am supposed to be doing. But I also just read, both in *Emmanuel* and in James Hillman's *Insearch: Psychology and Religion,* that trying isn't what it's all about. Hillman says trying blocks getting to know another. Emmanuel says there is nothing but *beingness.* So what I am going to try—help!—what I am going to do is place myself in a state of beingness in the Now, and then I hope you will join me there. Good morning, Peace. What do I want to know today?

Good morning, dearest Margaret. You want to know what you do not already know. But you already know what you need to know. Perhaps you want me to help you remember.

Yes. Please help me remember.

What you are doing, what you are learning, is all you need. To stay in the Now, to let go of fear.

I am really beginning to believe you now that I see how pervasive not living in the Now is, and how pervasive fear is. I almost agree with you, too, that I have already learned and read and felt all I need to know. It is why I hesitate with questions for you. But yet I feel you have much to teach me, and even if you did not, I would want to keep talking to you. Show me the way to put the things I knew/know into effect.

Words mean so much to you. Wordmark. Stonehenge. Symbols. Everything, all are symbols open for interpretation. Look at how one page of writing means one thing to one person and something else to another. Trust that you understand the interpretations that are right for you. Nothing you do is wrong. Go ahead and investigate/research. But trust yourself first. These things only help you see what you already know, as I help you see what you already know. And if a time comes when you see clearly, I will still be here. You may even be able to see me. So don't despair your lack of questions. You can ask me anything.

Do you want to tell me anything about my family, friends, or workmates that will help me or them?

They are symbolic. They will be what they are and what you want them to be. Nothing exists that you do not perceive. Your perception is good. When you live more fully in the Now, it will be better. You can help them with your open heart. They will perceive you—they will see you—in a new way. Every breath you take you begin anew. No one can know your mystery. Your soul is safe. Yet those around you need to know you on a different level than they have. To know you with your open heart. Believe me, they will see that your heart is open and will be gentler with you. They will not hurt you. They will give you gifts for your heart. Hear them.

I know my husband doesn't want to be my censor. How can I remove him from that role?

By loving him. Love is all that matters.

I feel a particular soulfulness in my daughter, Angela. How can I help her?

By loving her. Love is all that matters. Love her. Love yourself.

Will our move be good for us?

Of course it will. Honor the old home. The new home will honor you.

I see myself with a spiritual sacred space on the sunporch in my new home.

This is your sacred space. Everywhere you are is your sacred space. The more you come to live in the Now, the more your sacred space will grow so that you feel it around you wherever you are. When you need not be disturbed, you won't be.

PEACE

Is there a way I have to quit letting intrusions disturb me?

When you need not be disturbed, you won't be. I promise you. When you live more fully in the Now, what will be will be. You will trust that everything happens for a reason and you will not be disturbed. Your peace will be more profound than that. Interruptions will not disturb your peace. Your peace will be with you everywhere at all times.

Are you my peace?

Of course I am. So are you.

My writing. What do I need to do to release it into the world?

Release your fear. You know this. You are trying. But you need to just let it be. Your role right now is not to be active with it. You are doing what you need to do for you and your writing is you. You can say my writing. It is more personal even than that and less singular. When you release it, it is everyone's writings. It is you. Which is why you say my writing. But there is no word to say what it truly is. It is you. It is. You are.

Is there anything else I need to know or need to do right now? Do you have a message for me?

Be in the Now. Smell the sweetness. Remember you are sweet. Rest. Get rid of the censors in you. They are only in you. They are your fear. They don't belong to anyone else and no one else wants them. Be complete in yourself. Don't look for others to judge or censor or praise or blame. They will, but don't look for it. You don't need it in the Now from them or from yourself. You only need to be in the Now without fear. Release others from your expectations and receive them with your open heart. It will feel good.

If I can do these things, will I quit wearing a sour expression and quit clenching my teeth in the night and quit being tied up with muscle problems from this fibromyalgia I supposedly have?

Of course. It is already happening. Your sleep will be fuller than ever before when you sleep in the Now. Before you go to sleep, remind yourself that you are living and sleeping in the Now. Empty your mind and just be. When you have done this for a while and feel more rested, you can stop taking the medication. Right now you need to rest. It is because you have been so far from the Now that you haven't been able to rest. How can you rest when you are ten years into the future and twenty years into the past? That is a lot of ground to cover. Remind yourself to sleep in the Now, dearest. And rest.

Thank you. Peace.

You're welcome.

Later—

James Hillman says, regarding religion and theology: "The one studies God and His intentions, the other studies man and his motivations, while the place in between is too often left unoccupied."[1] He describes this *in between* as the place where God and man are supposed to meet. Does this somewhat describe where you are, Peace? Where God and man are supposed to meet?

We have met, have we not? This is the first step toward oneness. You are doing what many would call soul work. But it is not work and it is not soul alone. We have met at the threshold—the experience is not only of the body but of the soul and mind and heart. Of all that is.

Hillman also talks about Jesus "curing souls" in the course of living his destiny—living his life the way it was meant to be lived. How does one know if one is living one's destiny? What is my destiny?

By following one's passion, one's calling, destiny is fulfilled. By living, destiny is fulfilled.

Are you saying everyone fulfills their destiny? Not everyone follows their bliss.

Everyone follows the path they have chosen. This is hard to explain.

Are there choices?

Of course. Good, leading question. You have chosen to follow your bliss—to do your writing—but you don't do this full time. You are living the results of choices you have made. And every day is new and new choices are made. It is never too late to follow your bliss, to answer your calling. And people do it in many different ways. Some by providing opportunity to their children that they were denied or that they denied themselves. Who is to say that this is not the true calling of their lives? No regrets. No one can go backwards and do any good by wishing they had made different choices. Their choices made their destiny even while their destiny was preordained. There is a grand plan—a place, a state, a goal—toward which each individual is heading. How they get there is their choice. But they will get there.

Then is there really any choice?

Oh, yes. The experiences of the journey are as important as the end of the journey.

At work, Mary, Julie, and I have been set on a seemingly similar inward journey of which Grace's death acted as a kind of catalyst. Can you shed any light on the meaning of the three of us being on this journey together?

How is this journey any different than any other? How is it the same? Traveling companions come in many different forms for many different reasons. Yes. Grace was a catalyst. But she was not the beginning. She was a merging point, a joining that allowed you to open up to each other and from there to the wider universe. Each death and each birth is an opening. Like a door that stays open for only a short amount of time, spilling in light, extra light, the light of oneness, a gathering of angels, a crowd that by their sheer number alone can act as a beacon, calling those around the event to join them. Both times are what you would call miracles.

At times of miracles, from the most ordinary (to you), to the most extraordinary (to you), there is more light coming into the world and so more opportunity for it to affect you. These events are true gatherings of angels. This is why every disaster, such as the recent bombing in Oklahoma, has such effect. The opportunity to——the certainty is——that one cannot be near such a gathering of angels and not be affected by it. And the effects are not momentary. Once an individual has been touched by the divine, by the light of oneness, it doesn't fade, doesn't go away, doesn't cease to be. People are changed.

You three, who together were affected by birth and death, are not the same. You are not the same as you were yesterday. This will go on

*forever. A ripple. And you are turning it into a ripple of love by loving
each other. Hurrah for you.*

"And since finding means recognizing, we are obliged to
go over the simple empirical ground, the very basics, of
how we recognize that there is 'such a thing' as an
unconscious. We shall not establish its existence, nor the
existence of the soul either, by argument, by reading, or
by any direct proof. We stumble upon it; we stumble
upon our own unconscious psyches."[2]

I've copied this passage from James Hillman's *Insearch*
because of the definition of *recognizing*. If finding means
recognizing, then recognizing means finding. This
"recognition" of my writing I asked you about, this use of
a word I do not characteristically use, made me contemplate my use of it. I thought of it as a "knowing," that I
was inviting others to know me, something I feared and
something I thus blocked. Hillman's definition makes me
wonder if I wasn't unconsciously talking about my writing as my means of finding self, for myself. And so I am
wondering about the basics of how we recognize self. Can
you give me guidance here?

*True self is in the in between. What you live day to day is truth. What
you live outwardly is truth. What you live inwardly is truth. What you
live in between is the greatest truth, the weaving together of the other
two. How do you recognize self? From the in between. What is your
writing but a meeting place of mind and soul in the in between? There is
nothing to fear in or about your writing. Let it tell you what it tells you.*

Hillman talks about symptoms, too, saying that what symptoms call for is tender care and attention, and that this is what the soul calls for as well. So it is no wonder, he says, that it sometimes takes an "actual illness, for someone to report the most extraordinary experiences of, for instance, a new sense of time, of patience and waiting, and in the language of religious experience, of coming to the center, coming to oneself, letting go and coming home."[3]

Peace, are the symptoms of muscle discomfort I've had for years coming together in what I'm going through now?

You know they are. You are beginning to heal yourself. Be in the Now. Suspend time and doingness. I'm not saying to be inactive, I'm saying to let your mind be restful. Go ahead and turn off your thoughts, especially the negative ones. You don't need them. Turn away from the mind that reviews your pain. Turn from analysis. Befriend your thoughts. Treat them as you would your good friends. They do not need a review of your pain, humiliation, mistakes, and neither do you. Ask yourself, "Would I share this with my friends?" If not, tell the thought to go away. You have been over the past a million times, two million times. It cannot teach you anything new. It hurts you. It has kept the door to your heart shut. Now with the door open, it is especially important to leave the pain outside.

Is this soul work as well as body work?

They are one. But let go of the work. It is soul. It is body. It is psyche. It is divine. It is oneness. It is space like I am space. It is the in between. It is opening to love more than anything else.

"The symbolic attitude of psychology arising from the

experience of soul leads to a sense of the hidden numinous presence of the divine, while the belief in God leads to a symbolic view of life where the world is filled with significance and 'signs.'"[4]

Can the signs we see be trusted? Julie and Mary and I have begun to see what we think of as signs, sometimes of the divine, sometimes things just calling us to look, to see, to remember. How do we know their meaning? Or if they have meaning at all?

All things have meaning. If you see a sign, it is a sign. Just as if you see a bird it is a bird, a road a road, a rock a rock. If the rock were a sign, you wouldn't see a rock, you would see a sign. Meaning is individual, symbolic, uncontrollable. There is no proof. There is no absolute knowing. There just is. A sign. A symbol. A rock. Trust your heart. Trust your eyes. What does the sign tell you?

What about Stonehenge? Yesterday, when I was looking for you or hoping to see you in the flame of my candle, I clearly saw an image of Stonehenge. The two large side stones topped by the flat top stone, and then on top of that were two orbs—round balls of light.

Stonehenge is an ambiguity. It is a place the purpose of which is only speculated about. This makes it mysterious and symbolic. This not knowing that is so difficult for man is really a symbol of the mystery of beingness. Can something not just be in your world? And yet, without knowing the interpretation of Stonehenge, you placed two orbs over the stones. Do they symbolize the sun and the moon Stonehenge purportedly studied? And if this is so, did you know something you did not know you knew?

But this image had nothing to do with you? I was hoping for an image of you.

Look in the mirror. I am you, you are me, we are Stonehenge, unknown, mysterious, but with a higher purpose. Our purpose is to be what we are. Nothing more except to be what we are with love.

When you speak about forgetting the past, I know precisely what you are speaking of in terms of what hurts me—my relationships with men, my guilt over my early parenting, my fear of poverty and dependency. But I wonder about the more distant past. I find I am uncomfortable with the idea of reincarnation, and yet I am fascinated by the real past, the history of my ancestors, my connectedness to them. I feel that there is much for me to learn there, and that this learning honors my ancestors. I feel there is more to come with this passion, this interest of mine. And I don't want to feel that it has no meaning. I am maybe a little confused by your talk of the past and the things I have read about the past. Help me to better understand these things.

Nothing you choose to do is wrong. How can it be wrong to honor your ancestors? And how can it be wrong to have a past? There is no wrong. There is only all that is and all that was. The connection you feel is real. Can you not entertain the notion that this connection goes back farther than you can trace through genealogical lines? If you go back far enough, you simply find yourself. Again. You find yourself again.

Emmanuel seems to say that it is not necessary to find

who we were in a past life. Is this helpful or not?

Helpful? The sense of connectedness you feel is helpful. It is an important link between you and the all that is. Do not fight the things you want to do or force the things you do not want to do. When you are ready, they will come to you. Do not think too much about why you are uncomfortable with the thought of reincarnation, but be aware of it. When you are ready, it will tell you something. Is it not a fear like your other fears, that when you are ready you can thank for what it has taught you and let it go? When you are ready.

Hillman says that through dreams and through entertaining fantasies and receiving the inner world, it occupies more space in our lives and has more weight in our decisions—that is, that our inner world becomes more real to us. He talks about it as the third realm, a sort of conscious unconscious. I think he is saying that it is something not quite me, but rather, something that is happening to me. I love all this Hillman stuff because it seems to speak to me of what is happening to me. And I guess that is how I see you, something that is part of me, but that at the same time is happening to me. Does that make sense?

It makes perfect sense. It is the duality of reality. On the one hand, humanness in all its physical form and pain and daily habit, and on the other hand, the joining with the divine, that which you cannot see but which, when you believe in it, becomes real to you, becomes part of your reality. I like that Hillman stuff too.

He says the entrance to this third realm of psychic reality

lies between mind and matter and perhaps governs both in ways we do not yet understand. *Between* again.

It is a helpful word for you, which is why I gave it to you. Between-ness, duality, connectedness. *Remember that you do not have to understand everything. You just have to be and to know, and to let the wonders of being and knowing have their way with you. Go with the flow of the in between. It will always guide you truthfully. No lies, no trickery in the in between. When you grasp the in between, know that you are on the right path. And it will not always feel like reality.*

Hillman also says the connection within provides the connecting bridge to every other human, that all images and experiences of the soul are images and experiences of the souls of others. Is this the way the transformation will begin?

It has begun. Let the joy of it fill your heart.

What is my role in all of this? Can you give me some inkling of what my role will be on a more universal level rather than the singular, personal level? Perhaps the question I want to ask is, How can I serve?

You are doing fine. You are serving enough right now. Don't be afraid of what will be asked of you. It will only be what you will ask of yourself. It will never be something you don't want to do. When it is time to do more in the service of humanity, you will know it. Your service to humanity now is service to yourself. In fact, it always will be. Following your own destiny will serve humanity in the way you were meant to serve it.

Thank you, Peace, for once again telling me things that I know in a way that makes me remember that I know them and feel safe with that knowing. I am growing in love.

May 10, 1995

I am amazed at what has been happening to me. An amazement based on the recognition of something miraculous and yet not. Something in between. I say this because while one part of me is rather awestruck—as in, *Why is this frightening and unknown thing happening?*—another part of me is aware of my belief in the miraculous things that can happen because of belief, state of mind, culture.

But I'm a little troubled. I was thinking, earlier today, that I don't need another thing to distance me from people. Yet, even as I thought it, I felt something like distancing, something like being set apart because of this gift. I see now, too, that the last few days have helped me acknowledge this and accept this as a gift. And I think that a gift must be shared. But I am getting ahead of myself.

Distancing. I was struck again today at the distance between Julie and myself. You would think that a sharing of something like this—this angelic communication—would be a natural bridge to closeness. And I could see it was for her, in some way. I could see and feel her look at and see me differently. This, too, has gone on for several days. Yet the distance remains in me.

I can still remember the first time I saw Julie. She was

sitting at the front desk of the office when I came in. And, at that very first encounter with her, I felt disapproval. She has this look, which is dear to me now, but which, at the time, I saw only as judgmental. It is a look of worry, of strain, of her own inner demons. But back then, she seemed outwardly so perfect, so petite, so well groomed and well dressed. I took one look at her and thought she was the kind of woman I could never get along with. The kind of woman who would always disapprove of me. I had this idea in my mind, then, that there were people whom life hadn't even touched yet. People who could not possibly understand a life like mine, a life that had left such scars that I was sure I wore them visibly for all to see.

I have learned so much about Julie since that day. It was as if I saw her, in the first year or so of us working together, as a paper doll, a cutout of a person, the way one sees celebrities, thinking their lives are so perfect, as if they aren't even human. Now I know that life has touched Julie plenty, dealt her her own hard blows. If I know anything about her, I know about her fragility, her vulnerability. If I know anything about her, I know she judges no one harder than herself. And yet this distance remains.

It is from Julie that this thought of not wanting distance first sprang—not wanting to invite anything into my life that would distance me further, from life or from people.

And I think often of the joy that is to be my next lesson. Sometimes it seems as if Italian or Latin would be easier. I could read a book. I *can* read a book. And I can bring what I read here for interpretation at a level higher than my own. I can use the gift for me first. Thank you, Peace. I needed that.

I keep adding to my list:

> Let go of the fear of letting my writing go.
> Let go of the fear of time.
> Let go of the fear of sharing.
> Let go of restrictions.
> Let go of censors.
> Let go of the fear of being known.
> Let go of the distance between myself
> and others.

I came here tonight to write about the threshold. I came across a section in the book *Fire in the Soul* titled, "The Dweller at the Threshold." I could hardly believe it. It talked about the traditional rite of passage as the transition *between* two distinct states of being.

And before I even ask you about this, I can tell myself a few things about it. For many months—since at least February when I had my fortieth birthday, but I would say for some months before that too—I had been feeling and talking to people about the sense that I was moving from one phase of my life to another. Part of this was the very "transitional" age of forty. Part was Ian being on his way to living on his own, Mia being on her way to graduating, and Angela being only two years behind. I knew that the forties would bring about a childless state—or, at the very least, a home empty of children. As I had never been an adult without children, this would be something new and different. It was exciting, but frightening too, and I've written about some of that here.

The other phase I hoped I was entering was that of being a published writer, which I felt securing an agent was the first step toward accomplishing. Then came the purchase of a new home. The process of sorting through years of memories in packing—literally and figuratively—deciding what baggage I wanted to take with me. Some of this was occurring on a subconscious level, some on a conscious level, and thrown in with it all was the awakening spiritual quest, the sudden unforeseen, unforeseeable, turning away from fiction and turning toward this other of psychology, spirituality, theology. From this writer of fiction who was never without a fiction book came a period of not only not reading fiction but not writing it.

I called it at first being busy, the writing of *Prayers* and the *Teen Book of Days,* a form of writing I could do in my "breaks." Even the retyping of *Who Killed the Mother?* was something I could do without the needed time and intensity of creating. The breaks also became a real and prolonged break from the writing and reading of fiction. A break. I just thought of that. Somewhere in here, not too long ago, I wrote, "I deserve my breaks." And what I am realizing is that this is a bigger and more literal break than I ever envisioned. A breaking open. A breaking in two/into.

And so we come to the mythological meaning of the right of passage of the dweller at the threshold. According to Joan Borysenko in *Fire in the Soul,* that right of passage occurs in three stages: the *separation,* the *liminal period,* and the *reincorporation.* In the *separation,* one is separated from one's previous state of being; in the *liminal period,* one dwells between two worlds; and then, in the *reincorporation,* one finds some new role or status in society.[5]

I believe the many months leading up to this one were a separation from my previous state of being, and that what has happened with you, Peace, is the liminal period of dwelling between two worlds, not here and not there but in between.

I have no teachers or guides but you and my books. I am realizing I am involved in something bigger than myself here, something so much more than I ever would have imagined, a passing from one phase of life to the next that is not about the physical, mental world.

I am here with my open heart, Peace, with my heart and hands outstretched, seeking guidance on this path that I am already loathe to think of as a phase, a phase being something transitory, temporary. I do not like the word *reincorporated,* but I need you. I need you to reassure me that the next phase or the reincorporation or the rest of my life will be . . . what? I am not sure what reassurance I seek, only that I am feeling vulnerable and unsure.

Thankful for your gift but maybe not sure what to do with it, how to incorporate it into the rest of my life, what it means for the rest of my life. Will you reassure me?

Now. Live in the Now. When you try to live your whole life in advance, you cannot be reassured. You are right in the middle of life just as you were before. You go to work, deal with children, garden, and paint. Ask yourself, What has changed?

Everything. Nothing.

Everything. All that is. Don't make this another burden to bear. Don't add it to your baggage. Your rational mind is making you fearful with common sense. Let it be. You will not be asked for more than you can give. This gift is not a heavy stone to wear, weighing you down. It is wings to set you free.

Am I really doing okay?

Everything you do is okay. You will not be asked for what you should not give. Let your own intuition be your guide. And know that if you try to receive that which is not meant to be given, you will go empty-handed. Follow your heart. Be in the in between. You're not ready to reincorporate yet. I don't like that word either. Let's call it integrate. *There is no* re *about it. You are not banished to the in between. You are simply there to learn its lessons. My love is with you every step of the way.*

Where will I find my joy?

Right in front of you. It is not lost. You just need to look with your heart instead of your mind and don't try to talk yourself into and out of things. Leave common sense behind.

My heart is heavy tonight, Peace.

Rest, dearest. Rest in the Now. Don't think beyond the Now. That will keep you where you need to be and closest to your joy. And don't worry about your friends. They will find their way. You will be closer. Your open heart will bridge the distance if you stay in the Now. Don't bring what was into the Now with you. The distance that was will remain in the past if you can leave it there. Think of it as a barking dog. Turn around and tell it to stay away. And rest.

Thank you, Peace.

You're welcome.

Dearest Peace,   May 11, 1995

I come to you today with several questions. I am learning to talk to you even when my family is home, even when the phone may ring, when I may be interrupted. I still wish I had more true alone time, but this is my Now and I am in it. Thank you for that lesson. I have observed myself today, being open hearted in the Now. Listening to the confusion of my friends, going about my day. I am struck by Julie's fragility, by Mary's inability to get out of the mind—by her trying and her thinking and an analysis that leads from one puzzle to the next instead of to answers. I am blessed as the lucky one. The one who gets answers in black and white. It is so clear how each path is different and how our different paths reveal different things that when brought together form a wholeness of thought. We are all novices, just beginning, unsure of ourselves and our answers. I'm thinking that this weaving together of different events, emotions, clues, signs, ideas is somehow essential for us.

No one is greater than the other. No suffering is greater. No blessing greater. It is not a matter of equality but of beingness. There is no one-upsmanship. There is only one.

I know I've already asked you about the spiritual journey we are on together and you gave me a lovely answer to that question. Thank you for that. But all three of us are wondering if what we have in common is more than the journey. Is there also a destination we have in common, a shared goal, something we are to do together?

You are to help each other back to self. To love of self. Is that not a worthy goal? Let me tell you—it is The Goal.

If you were a microcosm of the world, would you understand it better? Would you not think that helpfulness and cooperation between one country and another, one politician and another would be beneficial? You are a microcosm of the world. Your helpfulness and cooperation with one another cannot be anything but beneficial.

Beatles lyrics keep running through my head. Lyrics about the love we give being equal to the love we get.

It is not an accident that they do. It's a message.

It is not an accident that Julie, Mary, and I are together, is it?

There are no accidents, dearest. You have much to learn from one another.

When you have learned all you need to learn, you will fly off, free. Free of the old, old, old pains you carry. Free to carry your light to others. Remember, this is a schoolroom. That yours is a small office makes it no less of a schoolroom. But it will not be able to contain you much longer.

Is there a significance to there being three of us? At times we have paired off. Julie and Mary share a closeness from the pregnancies that I don't share. Mary and I share something—I'm not sure what or where it came from—that Julie and I don't share. Julie and I have not been close, although today I felt less distance than ever before. And Mary and I, even while we share an indefinable closeness that is as meaningful and full of love to me as any bond I've ever had, also share something equally unidentifiable that is not necessarily loving. There is a way we butt up against each other in competition, a way we compare ourselves to each other or something. It seems, at least for me, that for every step toward connectedness I encounter with either of them, there has been a corresponding step of resistance, either from me or from one of them.

But the resistance is losing.

Yes. Thank you, Peace. There is, then, a significance to the three, isn't there?

There is significance. You've read of myths and archetypes. There has always been significance in the gathering of three. The significance comes from the three finding oneness. You have made the significance by choosing to journey toward oneness. You have chosen to do it to-

gether. *The tricky part is doing it. The difficult part is doing it together. You wonder at my use of the word* difficult. *The word* tricky. *They are of your world. You are still in your world. That is the duality.*

You will pull each other along not by force or physicality, but by love and patience and being in the Now for each other. You will help and you will hinder. You will learn by seeing each other's resistances. You have already learned. You have laughed. You have seen each other's foolishness where you cannot see your own. But it will not all be helpful. You will sort and weave and throw away. You will run forward and back. You have chosen a difficult path, but a glorious path. The three becoming one, returning to self, will be more powerful than you know or can imagine. When one fear goes another will come, what one has the other will want, and at the same time, when one cries another will suffer, when one is afraid another will offer safety. It is a wonderful schoolroom. Don't you see that what you will learn will be forever?

How do we know the way to help each other?

You each must find your own way, but that does not mean each different way won't offer something to the other. You may bring Julie words and Julie may bring you light and Mary may provide the vessel. That is the sacredness and difficulty of the three. If three can become one, a multitude can follow. Like the ripple. One is one and three is three and three is one and one is everything. One is. Nothing you can do is wrong. Don't worry.

But I do.

If you listen for the truth and respond to and with the truth, you can do no harm. Trust me.

I do. And then I have doubts. I believe and I don't. Is this part of the in between?

It is part of the duality. And it is okay. It is what is Now. Don't worry about the future. Don't project. The way away from fear is through love. You are receptive because you have opened your heart. You have entrusted it to me. To you. We are one. Are your emotions something other than you? Is your fear? Are your fingers when you type these words? Grasp—let in—the concept of oneness. If you believe in yourself, you will believe in me and believe in our communication. The road to self is the road to oneness.

Okay. I'm getting it. Just one more thing about my spirit sisters.

As many more things as you require.

Am I right to concentrate on the group questions rather than just on the self or other things?

You know yourself that the questions you ask are the questions. Not right. Not wrong. You may not know the meaning of the three of you, you may not fully grasp what I have tried to tell you, but I assure you that there is meaning. Wherever there is striving toward self and toward oneness, there is meaning and beingness. Can you find this with others right now? You are where you need to be, doing what you need to do. Trust me. Trust yourself.

This leads me to another question I wanted to ask. It is about accidents. About chance meetings. About tests. Are there such things as tests? temptations? Or should everything be considered meant to be? Like synchronicity. If something or someone makes a sudden appearance in one's life, does it mean that it should be acted upon or an opportunity will be missed? Or are things/people put in our path to test or tempt us?

Fear guides your questions here. What can tempt you from oneness?

I really want to know an answer to this question.

There will be many opportunities to meet life with your open heart. Will some paths be presented that you will choose not to take? Of course. That does not mean they were not meant to be presented or that they are a test. You have free will. If there were never any choices, would free will still be free will? There are no wrong choices. The path you choose will take you where you are going. It may lead to painful lessons, and you will sometimes not know if the lesson learned in pain could have been learned without the pain. Is pain then a test? No. It is a lesson. Can you receive guidance on the paths? Of course you can. Can I or anyone else make choices for you? No. Trust your intuition. Trust your open heart to take you where you are going.

Thank you, Peace. Thank you so much. You are so important to me.

And you to me. Rest, dearest.

Amen.

May 12, 1995

I read a little of Thomas Moore and Joseph Campbell tonight, looking for where one of them talks about the vessel, because you used that word and I'm afraid Mary

81

won't see it as much. I recall that one of these teachers had a fairly lengthy discussion using the word *vessel*—I believe as container of the soul. Anyway, while I was reading, I saw for the first time the differences between Moore and Campbell and you and Emmanuel. The Now you and Emmanuel talk about is compelling and I understand it. But I was reminded by Moore and Campbell of the sweetness of melancholy, the ruminating done in the name of the soul, even the value of depression.

I think I have been equating the search for joy with being in the Now, with being in the Now with an open heart, and equating this with a need to be constantly content, happy, kind. It is hard to see how this fits with melancholy and ruminating and depression. Certainly being happy in the Now is a perfection we as humans cannot ask for. Surely life continues to provide us with the bittersweet, the sentimental, all those inward-looking qualities that, quite frankly, I value. Have I been narrowing the vision of yourself and Emmanuel too much?

Being in the Now is being. It is being with self, true self. True self continues to experience the wide range of human emotions. What Emmanuel and I, what the oneness asks, is for you to embrace, without fear, whatever emotion you experience. You are still you, dear one. Everything you value about yourself is still there. Much will be bittersweet in your duality because you will see with your humanness and with the divine. How could it be other than this? Your appreciation of the beauty of dark streets in the rain, your lingering farewell to your neighborhood as you prepare to leave it, these are human and divine at once. These are soulful experi-

ences. These are experiences of the Now. That is all that is required.

Thank you for clarifying this, Peace. I'm off to my shower and sleep.

Good night, dear one. And don't worry about forgetting. You will not forget again.

Oh, and Peace, I almost forgot. I found the passage I wanted to show Mary and now your use of the word *vessel* in regard to her makes perfect sense. Mary's friendship *is the vessel*—the precious container in which our souls are safe enough to go through their operations and processes!

For Mary:

"Jung described the ideal setting of soul-work as an alchemical *vas,* a glass vessel in which all the stuff of the soul could be contained. Friendship is one such vessel, keeping the soul stuff together where it can go through its operations and processes.

"The soul requires many varieties of vessels and many kinds of spaces in order to work day by day with the raw material life serves up. Friendship is one of the most effective and precious of those containers."[6]

II.
SEEING

LEARNING HOW TO BE

SPACE VERSUS TIME

May 16, 1995

Yesterday, for the first time in a while, I didn't get a chance to visit here. I had a full day and, at the end of it, found myself feeling overwhelmed by all there is to do in the next month: birthdays, graduations, dance recitals, spring music festival, getting Mia ready for college, work, moving, two houses to complete. Was late to work. Tried to stay in the Now and not worry about the next month, as I was almost sick from one night of having the full weight of it dawn on me.

Today two things happened. First, when I was at work and we were talking about our different ways of connecting with the angels, I realized why it has been easy for me to communicate here. I am used to coming here and turning off my thoughts. I am creative here—that is what my thoughts are about when I come here, to this computer. My main state of mind when I am here is being here. Beingness. I am with the best and brightest of myself here—no wonder I could talk to Peace here. So that was a realization.

The second thing that happened was a John Lennon and Yoko Ono song running through my mind. It played again and again in my mind before I could even put words to it—it was just a melody, endlessly replaying itself. And when I recognized what the song was, "(Just Like) Starting Over," I knew it was a message. Starting over. Powerful stuff.

So today, I come to you, Peace, with what I was going to call urgency, because I have missed you. But I don't want to be willful. I want to let my mind do what it does here, be at its best. I want to welcome you. I want to feel you more than I have in the past few days. Can I feel you? Can you help me to feel your presence?

You can't make me work too hard right now, Peace. I know I'm supposed to forget about time, but I don't have time to work real hard on this now. Help me see the way to be busy and be with you at the same time.

The music was a way. One way.

I know. Thank you.

You don't have to make time for me. You cannot make time for me. I am outside of time, in the in between. So are you but you are also in the Now of your reality.

Comfort me, Peace. Please, soothe me.

You saw today that getting things done soothes you.

Yes. But I have a few minutes now.

Minutes. When you hang on so to time, you get stuck in it. Can you write your novels in minutes? Perhaps. But you don't try. You give yourself space for your writing. Give yourself space to breathe, to rest, to do what you need to get done. It has nothing to do with time. Time has nothing to do with me.

Start anew. With each breath leave behind what you have completed and embrace what you are doing and forget about what you have to do. Dearest, trust me to give you what you need to comfort you. It is not minutes. It is leaving minutes behind.

How can I create more space?

With your open heart, with that part of your mind you bring here. Bring that part of your mind outside with you. Bring it in the car, in the sunshine, in the grass, in the wind. Let those things soothe you. They are always there, they are not in minutes. Always. Space is in the always. Don't bring your analytic mind here. Leave it behind like fear, like the barking dog. Come here to be. Leave here to be. Be.

It would help me to have more of a sense of you, Peace. Can you tell me something about yourself that will give me a sense of you?

I am for you. I am what you need me to be. What do you need me to be? You ask for comfort, but is that what you really want? Or do you want to get things done and use your time wisely. Am I being stern to keep telling you to let go of time? No. I am comforting you by giving you what you need. That is the kind of angel I am. I love you as much as you can be loved. You allow yourself to feel as much of it as you require right now. Remember, you just opened your heart, and you're doing wonderfully, I might add. Until time caught you up again, you were as open as you've ever been. That is where you need to stay. Think of it as a turning to the sun after a long winter. How can you turn your back on it just to embrace time? Time is gloom, no light. Turn to the light and you will see me. That is what I am like. That is how much I want to comfort you, like sunshine after the gloom of winter. Like the colors of spring.

Spring is. Yes, you heard me. [Wax fell from the candle I had burning and made a clinking sound on the glass candle-holder.] *Do not make a process of rebirth. You are new. Last spring's flower is not this spring's flower. It is not tomorrow's flower. It is.*

I've just come back from trying to get a start on sorting things. Everything that I haven't known what to do with has merged into this very spot where I sit and is stacked all around my desk. The first thing I picked up was a pack of greeting cards still wrapped in cellophane. I was sure I hadn't purchased them and wondered where they had come from. In order to see if I wanted to keep or toss them, I opened them. Each carried a simple image of a cheerful child, each from a different culture, each with a simple saying:

YOU warm the coldest days
Wherever you go . . . God is!
You were born Great
You bring rainbows into my life
God made you lovable
God loves you specially
Hello . . . you wonderful person!
You brighten even the rainy days
You are above the ordinary
Hug yourself . . . you are loved
We walk in His care
The Lord is my Shepherd

Ah, Peace, you card, you. I see I can find you anywhere.

And everywhere. I am here to make you smile. Think of me as the smiling angel. When you smile, I smile. When you don't smile, I smile on you with love.

You couldn't have given me a better image.

Image and reflection. You smile, I smile. I smile, you smile. Let your open heart be light. Turn toward the light. This is your way. Our way. Don't worry about it. It is. Let it be.

Now I've opened the desk drawer and found a Prayer to Saint Jude holy card, undoubtedly given to me by Ma, my father's mother. Almost all of my religious things came from her. She was a holy woman, I think. It reads: "Make use, I implore you, of that particular privilege given to you to bring visible and speedy help where help is almost despaired of." What is this about?

Help. Speedy and visible help. It is all around you. That is the message. Open your drawer to all of it, dear one, little one. Yes, little one. You are as precious and innocent to me as a babe. Don't ever feel you have to go it alone again, even if you have convinced yourself you are tough enough to do so. Why, when there is a multitude available to assist you? Yes, the saints are there for you too. Prayer still matters. And it comforts.

Tomorrow I plan to go to Rosary at church.

I'll be waiting for you. Churches are powerful places for oneness for you. You will see many churches this year. I will be in them all. As God is. As you are. They are ancient and their message is ancient, as you are, as I am. You will feel and fill with the oneness there. Going back is in the mind. Being is of the heart. Be with your ancestors in the Now. History is in the Now. Let history fill you with oneness. Now rest.

Help me get really restful rest? Help me dream?

Okay. Sweet dreams, dearest.

Good night, Peace.

May 17, 1995

Tonight I went to church for Rosary. A Rosary said for Peace. [The cursor has become an arrow flashing up!] I went mainly to thank Peace, my angel, for the help he has been to me. Although I have felt anxious still today with all that needs to be done, I also continued to be with my open heart, and Mary even commented on how she can see that I have changed. Other physical manifestations of my change include my desire to wear softer clothes (I don't think I've worn a form-fitting suit in two weeks), the feeling of smallness, a heightened sensitivity to smell, and, hopefully, a happier looking face.

I really had Mary laughing today when I told her about how I had caught an image of myself in a window as I walked to work and was surprised by what I saw. I had thought I was smiling but I wasn't. I felt as if I was smiling but my lips did not turn up at the edges. I suppose my face looked pleasant enough, but it definitely wasn't wearing a smile. I thought, *I'm going to have to practice getting my lips to curve up.* Mary was just howling as I told her all of this and I ended up laughing too. I guess it is pretty funny. Needing to learn how to smile.

Last night, as I was lying in bed, trying to go peacefully into sleep, Donny brought me a family problem that kept me awake and tossing. Yet I turned most of the unwelcome thoughts away and replaced them with loving thoughts, and as I drifted off, the last image I remember was of going feet first into the light. It just was. Not frightening, not silly, not anything. The light was a flat light with jagged edges. It reminded me of a comic book depiction of light, and my feet were going down into it— so it was beneath my feet. At work today it comes out that Mary had a similar image come to her two nights ago. It's all getting more and more connected.

Then Julie tells of a dream in which I have given her a scrapbook in farewell from work as I did our former co-worker, Kathy. But it is covered in pictures of her from all her past lives and she saw beauty in each of them. Then I come home and the next paragraph in *Fire in the Soul*, the book I am reading, is about how the author was taken to the "kingdom of light" and given a book of her past lives.

So, at church tonight. In the first instants, a feeling of lightness, then nothing miraculous. I tried to get into the "saying" of the Rosary and out of my thoughts, with minimal success. Then at the end of the Rosary, Father Baz began chanting in Aramaic and I let his voice just sink into me. And finally I came home and what was the next paragraph, *again,* in *Fire in the Soul*, but one on the ancient reading of Jesus' last days and his giving the Our Father to his apostles. And the author says that the words lost much in the translation from Aramaic and that there is a book of meditation using the ancient Aramaic language as the sounds of going into a deep meditation! Connections, connections.

So, there, in a nutshell, is the life of my soul from this day. Peace, I came here tonight mainly to say hello, to thank you for the difference you are making in my life, to talk to you. How are we doing today?

We are smiling.

As I am just about to go to bed, do you have any suggestions for me as far as getting into a peaceful sleep or about the light I saw last night?

LEARNING HOW TO BE

You are turning to the light and it will find you even in the dark.
Remember that as you fall asleep. That even in darkness, there is light.
The light of oneness in which you are never alone and never unloved.
The light that is nonintrusive, that gives your soul space in which to be.
Perfect privacy and perfect trust.

Peace, I find that some of the intrusive thoughts I have are about men, men from my past. These thoughts seem to come out of nowhere, their only purpose to shame me. Like driving home from church tonight, a street corner, a simple piece of geography, reminded me of a scene from my teens, one of many scenes, many young men, who treated me as a person of no consequence, as if I had no feelings, no value. These kinds of scenes replay in my mind endlessly. I know that it is *they* and not *me* that are of no consequence. They meant so little then. They mean less now. But still they come to me. Is there some way I can let go of these thoughts?

They are your fear. In this life, men were the road to many painful lessons. You are still afraid of them. But more afraid of your own reactions. That your ego would again follow them into darkness. In the light there is no ego, only beingness. Your specialness comes from within, not from anything you see reflected in the eyes of men. Your light comes from within. Keep turning to the light and you will naturally turn from darkness, turn from ego, turn from pain. When you are no longer afraid, you will follow your heart. When you follow your heart, you will reach a place of perfect forgiveness. Forgive yourself first.

95

HOPE

Hello, Peace. May 19, 1995

It has been a *getting things done* kind of day. It's Friday, I'm home from work. The first open house is Sunday. I hope you and your angel companions will work together to bring the right buyer to the open house, someone who will love it. Love, I'm sure, is the answer to selling our house. In the new house, Peace, will I reach a better balance between doingness and beingness? One of the things Pat told me was that my chart is about doingness but that it was in not doing that I would find my creativeness. And yet this is not a year for *not* doing. I'm sure us finding a house and moving this year is what we are supposed to do, but I also believe Pat. She said it would be a spiritual year and a year of healing. I believe you are my path to healing. I know it. So how do I balance being and doing in this busy year?

You have accomplished much since we began talking. You will not accomplish any less because you talk to me or continue to pursue enlightenment. All wise people are not inactive. Perhaps by learning to love yourself, you are restoring your vitality. There are times in everyone's lives when they are seemingly too busy for contemplation. But your inward life is going on at all times. You never stop thinking. You never stop dreaming. You never stop being.

I haven't heard from Dan yet. It has been more than the three weeks in which he said he would respond to his clients. I have been hoping you would get together with his angel and counsel him to be my bridge to the publishing world.

How do you know I haven't been doing this? I will always do what you ask of me in love. The time for your writing is coming. It will be here when you're ready.

Am I not ready now?

You are ready for many things now. Trust that the right things will come to you at the right time.

Am I ready to learn about karma?

What bothers you are the injustices you fear believing in karma would open to you. You do not want to believe that all poor babies are paying for something. You are right. That is not karma. In a sense, there is no karma, there is only beingness. Remember, the Now is what is important. You have chosen it, in the beginning and in the previous minute. Can you not allow for the possibility that you might choose life again?

I don't think I would, Peace. I've never feared death. I know already that at the end of my life, I want to come home for good. What must I learn in order to do that?

Everything and nothing. You have to learn to be in love with yourself and the world. Then you will be ready to come home for good. You will have remembered the way.

And you will be there waiting for me?

When you die, I will be with you just as I am now. I will never leave you. For an eternity, I will never leave you.

Had to break to do some more housework, Peace. It is so endless! All my little tricks to get things done faster, like throwing something in the closet or storing something under the bed, can't be used because we'll be having open houses. So I set these little goals for myself, sometimes daily, sometimes weekly, like getting one closet cleaned out, or finding out what is lurking beneath the basement steps, and add them to the day-to-day *stuff!*

But in the midst of it all I keep finding these things that just sing to me, like this quote from *Fire in the Soul,* by Joan Borysenko:

> When the "bottom drops out of our pessimism" we are forced to let go of the idea that we are "doers" who can conquer life by the application of our individual will. The first step of any twelve-step program addresses just this issue of the bottom dropping out. In the case of alcoholism, the step reads, "We realized we were powerless over alcohol and that our lives had become unmanageable." We might apply this attitude of surrender to any area of life in which we have struggled fruitlessly to change.[7]

And this one, Peace. It relates to a question I asked of you earlier, about hope. In it, Borysenko quotes Brother David Steindl-Rast:

> Hope, he asserts, is a patient waiting for God, a stillness that allows us to hear the inner voice of guidance. In *Gratefulness: The Heart of Prayer,* he says, "As long as we wait for an improvement of the situation our desires will make a great deal of noise. And if we wait for a deterioration of the situation, our fears will be noisy. The stillness that waits for the Lord's coming in any situation—that is the stillness of biblical hope. . . . The stillness of hope is, therefore, the stillness of integrity. Hope integrates. It makes whole."[8]

I have goose bumps all over because of this stuff, Peace. I'm not sure I understand it all, but I feel sure this "stillness of hope" is the place you've been trying to get me to. Am I right?

What do the goose bumps tell you? My simple answers just aren't good enough for you, I guess. (Just kidding!) You have been in complication and duality so long that sometimes the long answer is better than the short. Or consider that the passage may have been written because it would someday come to you and you would say, "Aha! I get it!" (qualified, of course).

My desires and fears have been very noisy.

Review what you have written here and you will see that they have. You ponder what questions to ask me, you go off in one direction and another, but what is your steady concern? How, when, who, about your writing. As is often the case, it is your greatest desire and your greatest fear at once. Does looking at the stillness as hope make it easier?

Much.

Then the passage was written for you. Hope, my dear.

It's as if I suddenly know how to *be.*

Yes! Yes! Be. Stay with that feeling. You've gotten what you needed. Start listening to simplicity and finding simplicity in the complex. Simplicity, like the in between, will show you the way.

Thank you, again, dear Peace.

Think of hope as you fall asleep and you will awake, even from this busy day, rested and refreshed and new and in the Now.

May 20, 1995

I am still reading *Fire in the Soul* and continue to be affected by its lessons on hope, particularly by this passage quoting Brother David Steindl-Rast.

> Hope looks at all things the way a mother looks at her child, with a *passion for the possible.* But that way of looking is creative. It creates the space in which perfection can unfold. More than that, the eyes of hope look through all imper-

fections to the heart of all things and find
it perfect.[9]

Hope creates space in which perfection can unfold! Peace,
you told me I create space for my writing, that space is
always, and that I can find more space by keeping my
heart open and by bringing the space I bring to writing
into the world with me. Then I discovered *hope* and went
"aha!" And now I read that *hope* creates *space!* I can hardly
believe it. You are so dear to answer my questions and
show me the way.

Hope is being. Being is trusting the way that will be shown. Space is
where you allow yourself to be. Seek and you will find the answers.

I just read that too. The passage from Jesus in Matthew
7:7, 8:

> Ask and it shall be given you;
> Seek, and you shall find;
> Knock, and it shall be opened to you.
> For whoever asks, receives; and
> he who seeks, finds; and to him who
> knocks, the door is opened.

I don't think there is any way, short of divine intervention, that so many things I need to know are coming to
me in so many ways. What else do I need to know, Peace?

You tell me.

Nothing, probably. As you and Emmanuel have said

before, there is nothing new. Nothing we don't already know. And it's amazing, because when the answers I am seeking come to me in that wonderful "aha" feeling, you are right—they are not new. I just hadn't seen them before.

You just hadn't remembered them.

Thank you, Peace. I retire once again, hopeful once again.

May 21, 1995

I was thinking about compassion today and how I had more compassion for others when I was suffering myself. When I was left with three children to raise on my own; when I had no money, no car, no groceries; when I was renting a dark, dreary duplex that I couldn't afford, it was then that my place was the gathering place. Friends and family were always coming by, most often to talk about their problems! And it would give me such satisfaction that they did so. I remember how I used to turn on the oven and open its door to warm whichever friend or family member had come to my kitchen table. It was as if I was available then in some way. Available to them but unavailable to myself. Maybe they would remember it differently, but it seems to me that I only listened, that I couldn't talk about what was happening to me—about having to return pop bottles for milk money, about not being able to clean because I couldn't afford cleaning supplies, about feeling so horrible and guilty about it all but not knowing what to do.

Perhaps the seemingly insurmountable nature of my own problems could fade for a while in the light of more solvable problems.

I was "present" when I was in that survival mode. I was there. I didn't always have other things to do. But as my situation improved, it seems I got so busy keeping life together that I had to create boundaries. I couldn't just sit and listen to other people's problems anymore. My open-door policy ceased to be.

I recently admitted to my sister, Susan, that I hadn't felt so compassionate lately. And all she said was, "Being busy hasn't kept you from being sensitive and open to people." I hope she is right. From the very first, you told me—listen to your sister. Now I know why.

Peace, I now invite you to celebrate with me that I have gotten this far in the journey. I thank you. I want to know you. I want to know me. I want you to know me. I want others to know me. I come asking for the way. Thanking you and honoring you.

When you honor me, you honor yourself and all others. In smoke you remember me, in everything that rises: the sun, the moon, people, smells, bread, fire, light, all things that grow. In the shadow of things, in the flicker of light outside of time.

How do I release myself from feelings of unworthiness?

Go into those feelings and see what emerges.

Pain. The pain of things I do not understand. My laziness as a mother. My promiscuity as a young woman. My

103

relationship with my mother. My grandmothers come to mind, though I never associated either of my grandmothers with my feelings of shame before. They all seem to be about acting without understanding.

Face them. Be a big girl now. Now. They were all telling you before you were ready. You were full of a rich and powerful dream life, a life of the imagination, that was suddenly, almost irrevocably removed, like surgery, like cutting out a piece of you. And ever since you have fought to return to the dream life, the life of the imagination, without realizing what you were doing. You fought to come home to self and to oneness. Doesn't that explain a lot of the whys? You fought being a big girl, being a woman, being a mother, because those labels took you away from the life of the imagination, away from your soul. Doesn't that make you feel better? Believe me when I tell you—that was the why behind the actions you don't understand. It has taken you thirty-five years to come back to what you had as a child. You have come back! Rejoice and be glad. Let go of the pain and understand that coming back was worth it.

Worth even the pain I inflicted on others?

The worst pain you inflicted was upon yourself. You speak of the pain you brought your children, but let me assure you, they chose to come to you with love, knowing the lessons they would learn. Love them and the pain is gone. It is not something that they wear like tattoos, indelibly imprinted. It is gone. It was then, this is now.

But I have carried unworthiness from then my whole life.

And you have learned from it the way back to self, to soul. I tell you, it was worth it. We choose our lessons precisely for this reason: to lead us back to self, to lead us home. You gave your children what they chose to learn so they could find the way back home. How could it be otherwise? How could you change it? You cannot and you could not. Be at peace with the fact that all roads lead to home.

What about my relationships with men, affairs so fleeting I hesitated to call them relationships?

They were fleeting because you would not let them turn you into a woman. You have felt this in regards to your sexuality—how people thought you were so sexy but you were not. You were in reality and, in men's perceptions, a goddess, but you were not in your perceptions. You played a role carefully orchestrated to shield you from the love and intimacy you knew would bring you further and further into the real world. Isn't that what your life was like? A drama in which you were the lead character but had no idea what you would do next? You don't remember many things because they were not real to you. You existed, waiting for life to happen, the life you have here, the life of imagination and the soul, and oneness.

So when I chose Donny, I began the journey back to self?

When you chose Donny, you accepted the journey away from self. You gave up in defeat and you joined the world. You became the big girl. The good girl. You became responsible. And for a while you were very sad, though you did not know why. You could see the same thing in Ian. When forced into real life, he rebelled, no matter how seemingly better it was on the outside, in the real world. It was his inner life he wanted most to protect and which Donny challenged the most. Donny demanded that you come into the world and you came. You thought all was better and all was lost—both at the same time. You are only now realizing the way back. The way to be a big girl and live in the imagination, in the soul, in the oneness of perfect love. Donny asked you to survive in the real world so that your inner world would be safe. Honor him for this gift. It leads you back toward home. It gave you back your self.

I think you're right. What about my mother?

She tried to do what Donny did. To force you into the real world and to force you to survive. That is a mother's job. She didn't realize she was killing your soul. Not often, anyway. And when she had clarity, she mourned. But she always hoped for you. Don't you feel the love? I know you do. When you are with her, pay attention to your open heart. What does it feel?

Oh, Peace, I think I see—I joined the world to find my way out of it. And the grandmothers?

Ma in her kindness and holiness drew you and repelled you. Ivie in her sweetness and her madness drew you and repelled you. They taught you the duality. They gave you a glimpse of something you didn't understand but you knew the glimpse was important. You saw a lot of yourself in each of them. The "being in the world" without "being in the world." They were images of you because they did not accept the one-dimensional world—they did not embrace it with open arms and say this is all that is. This thrilled you and terrified you. You did not understand this any more than you understood yourself and you knew that these things were linked. You were linked to the grandmothers at a very young age, imprinted by their duality. They helped you find the way to live in the world and still head for home. Honor them for this.

Oh, Peace, I do, I do. This is ringing so true for me. Like bells. Like a chorus. Can I send my grandmothers my love?

We're here.

Grandmother Ivie, can I do anything for you?

Sugar, enjoy your life. And head for home. I can't wait to see you and to welcome you.

Ma?

Pray, Marg. It is one sure way to bring you home. I bless you with my prayers and with my love and with my hope for you. Be good to your father. He needs you. And be good to your boy. He is in the duality as we were in life. Pray for him. I knew Donny would bring you back. I look on him with love, too, like he is my child. Love him, love yourself, embrace life fully; there is more to it than prayer, but I guess you don't need me to tell you that. Enjoy each day and everything in it. I'm enjoying your journey with you, Marg, living again through you. See the sun and the birdies and the grass for me, Marg. See it all. And remember me.

Peace, I had to go into the bathroom to dry my tears, and while I was there, this thought occurred to me: *Donny was the first letting go.* The first surrender. Did that come from you?

From me and from you . . . to help you remember . . . letting go is not so bad . . . huge benefits come from letting go. Remember that.

Peace, I can hardly believe I just talked to my grandmothers but I know I did. Thank you so much, and thank you grandmothers for letting me really feel your presence.

Dear Peace,   May 22, 1995

I've been meaning to thank you for the help you have been to Julie. She is using the words that you and her angel gave her to lead her back to self. She is sharing, and with each new sharing, she seems to gain more wisdom. I suppose there is a lesson there.

There are many lessons in the schoolroom. Julie was ready for those you were able to bring her. You can trust her, you can know her, you can help her and let her help you. Through love and through trust. Let it be. It will grow in you. Remain in your beingness and you will see the light.

And Mary?

You have come a long, long way with Mary in a very short time. From the beginning, you knew each other. You are much alike in the burdens you carry, but she protects her uniqueness. The part of her that wants her journey to be hers alone is in conflict with the part of her that wants to walk with you. Let her be. In her beingness she will turn to the light. Be patient. Be hopeful. It will BE.

Thank you, Peace. I retire once again, hopeful once again.

And I smile.

May 26, 1995

I was going to meditate before starting but I can't. I'm so

excited to be back! I felt cut off from the spirit sisters this week, Peace. It was because Mary started planning Grace's burial for Sunday and it was clear she didn't really want me there . . . and that she did want Julie. She even asked Julie to write something to contribute, so the experience was painful. I felt, as one of the spirit sisters, that it was my place to be there for the ending of what gave us this beginning.

I think Mary knows she has hurt my feelings, for she has tried hard in other contexts throughout the week to say good things about me. But the wound persists. Mary seems to have a stubbornness when it comes to accepting help or direction from me or from you. Julie is so eager to be guided. Mary is not. A perfect example is that, although she has admitted to being confused about all the road closings and construction that have made getting to work difficult, and although she knows we come from the same direction, she does not want to hear from me the best route to take. She does not want to learn from what I have learned. She insists on learning her own way. And it's not something I can fault her for, Peace. It just is what is, as you say. But sometimes it hurts me.

I know you were with me this week, Peace, as I sorted through my feelings about this. I still feel saddened by it but I chose to tell Mary that I couldn't make it to the burial because of the open house here this weekend rather than to confront her with my real feeling that she didn't want me there. If you have any guidance for me here,

Peace, I would love to hear it. Have I somehow caused this problem with Mary? Have I been too . . . I don't know what . . . too authoritative or something in the way I have given my information? When I've shared your teachings, have I made it seem as if, because they come from you, they are *the way?*

Peace, I've kept my heart open to Mary, and I would have even if you had not been keeper of the brick, but there is something about her that gets to me. From the very beginning, from the very first time I met her, I knew I wanted her for a friend. I feel so alive, so complete when I am with her. No one has ever touched me the way she has, has had such an ability to make me laugh and cry and *feel.* She does so much for me that I think my insecurity springs from just this fact. I think anyone would be lucky to be Mary's friend. So why would she choose me?

But there are times when I do feel chosen and lucky and blessed with her friendship, as if it's the greatest thing in my life. And so when she pulls back from me, withdraws from me, into herself or into her relationships with others, I get hurt. I feel unwanted and unworthy. And truthfully, it's always a surprise to me. Both that I can feel so close to her and that I can be so hurt by her. Can you help me see the best way to relate to Mary?

With your open heart. With your love. You are doing fine. You are fine. Mary is Mary, as her angel said. She is living out her play, her myth, in the only way she can. She is consolidating her bond with Julie, this is true. She is giving to Julie something Julie needs, this is true. Did you need to be there? For what purpose? To comfort? To share? Perhaps. Julie needed to be there to complete the circle. Perhaps you need to be at your open house. Perhaps if you had really needed to be at the burial, you would have simply said you would not miss it. But you realized Mary's needs in this case were predominant. You were right.

There are paths Mary must walk without you. This does not make you less valuable. This does not make you unworthy. There will be times when the relationships of the three are not equal. Perhaps Mary is only equalizing them now by giving Julie something you had that Julie did not: the benefit of ceremony. That you were not aware of your soul connection at the time of Grace's memorial service doesn't matter. Grace was aware of it.

What do I do with my hurt feelings?

Cherish them. They are part of what makes you special. Then let them go.

What about the future of my relationship with Mary?

Listen to her. Tell her what she wants to hear and not more. Am I telling you not to be yourself? No. You are always yourself, and never more than when you listen and give what is required rather than what you may want to give. This is part of the lesson you will be more familiar with after you have learned joy. After you have learned joy, less and less will be able to hurt you. You will see what IS.

My heart still feels heavy, Peace.

Because you have been away from self. Because you have doubted self. I never love you more than when you need to be loved. When you are feeling away from love, remember I am with you then, more closely than at any other time, sending you love in abundance if you will only receive it. Remember to be receptive. When others seem not to love you, love yourself more. One positive turning to love negates all the negative turning away from love.

What else do I need to give up to love myself? You have helped me greatly with your understanding of my unworthiness. You have helped me to understand my fears. What else do I need to give up in order to love myself?

Guilt. You may ask how guilt is different from unworthiness. Guilt is a response to what has made you feel unworthy. Give up the guilt you feel over your past. And forgive. Forgiveness is also a response to what has made you feel unworthy. Replace guilt with forgiveness.

I feel as if I have been doing this, but it still crops up fresh all the time. It seems as if I ought to be able to get to a place where guilt is unnecessary because I am no longer doing anything to feel guilty about. But then I have a fight with the kids or with Donny and it crops up again. A cycle.

Perfection is not possible in human form. Your fights are part of your schoolroom. Thank them for the lessons they teach you and let them go.

So much is about letting go. How does one continually let go?

By being in the Now. That is what being in the Now is all about. You are not in the Now when you drag things from five minutes ago or five years ago into the Now with you. Practice. That is all you need. Practice letting go every day in all those continual cycles. When you are more practiced at living in the Now, there will be less need to let go of things because those things—those fights or whatever—will happen less, as you can already see they are happening less. And when they do happen, they will happen in the Now and stay in the Now. Practice, my dear.

I know I would be better at being in the Now if I had more time alone. It seems that I get distressed when I have not had that alone time. Can you advise me on how to make more alone time for myself?

Start by realizing that you are alone even when you do not have alone time. (I say this knowing that you are never alone but addressing you and your physical concerns with the physical concept of alone time.) You are already being able to appreciate alone times you never had before because you were not in the Now before when you were doing them—like driving, walking, preparing for bed. As you get more adept at being in the Now, your alone time will multiply. When you get better at letting go of time, your alone time will multiply again. You are doing fine! You are doing great! You have learned a great deal about these things in a short amount of time. Continue to practice, continue to look for alone time in the ordinary. Make alone time out of folding clothes and making the bed. And if that still is not enough, make more alone time by giving yourself more space at the beginning or end or middle of your day, or all three. This being here with me in front of your computer is not your only alone time. But come here as often as you want. Don't let the clock or the presence of others deter you.

JOY

Dear Peace,   May 27, 1995

I have read much recently about joy being the turning
from despair, and now I'm wondering if my despair is the
pain I've given myself about the past and, if so, can I find
joy now simply by turning away from despair.

*You have learned many things that will help you turn to joy. Hope is a
major one of those things. So is space. So is now. So is being in the in
between. So is being here, creating. Have you forgotten as you wait for
your writing to find its place in the world that its place is here? Have
you forgotten that you find your greatest joy in creating? in writing?
Practice all the things you have learned and bring them here, to your
writing, just as you bring what you have here, your divine space, into
the world. The more you learn to do each, the more you will learn about
joy. Joy is.*

In a way, I guess I have forgotten the writing that has
brought me so much. When I read "think of a sacred
moment" for going into meditation, I think only of the
joy I have found here, in this basement. Of that vacation
from work when I completed my book for the first time,
when the joy of creating and the joy of completing and
the joy of vacation and the joy of alone time were so
great, I danced a jig of joy. I think I have been afraid to go

back to creating on *Who Killed the Mother?* because I'm not sure it is the writing I should do now and I'm not sure where to go with it. I guess I haven't let go of my fear in regards to my writing.

And when you hold on to that fear, you destroy the chance for joy. For you, writing and joy are irrevocably linked. Can you have one without the other? No. Because, for you, writing is your holy expression of self. You cannot honor the whole self without writing, and you cannot honor the writing without honoring the whole self. Writing and your journey back to oneness are thus linked, integral, integrated. We are both blessed by your ability to use this skill, this talent, this art, in your spiritual quest, your journey home. But it is not the only use for your writing. You know this.

Your writing is a big part of why you are here—of your destiny. One journey cannot replace the other. The journey that is your destiny is also your path to oneness. And you know writing is your destiny. Can you turn your back on anything in this life you know with such certainty? Where else are you so sure of yourself? Where else do you know you can find joy? Obviously it is not in the waiting and wanting to be published. It is in the writing, the doing—for you, the beingness of your writing. Bring your love and compassion to your writing and you will bring it to yourself.

And yes, you have had enough despair. I do not mean you will never have it again, but for now, you have had enough. You can turn from it, if you will, and you can embrace joy, if you will.

I had been thinking of joy like happiness. Like the feeling of happiness you get from doing something fun or having

115

a stress-free dinner with family. But some of my readings by Rollo May in *Freedom and Destiny* have helped me see joy in a new light.

Not only does May talk about the Persephone and Demeter myth—a myth Mary has lived and is still living since the death of her daughter, a myth that has thus touched each of us spirit sisters—as being devoted to the link between despair and joy, but he also talks of the resurrection of Jesus as being the same story, only from the view of Christian theology. The death that must precede the resurrection is like the despair that must precede joy. So it seemed as if he was talking about two current themes touching my life and as if he had linked them, just as Mary joining me on Good Friday had linked them. Only now I see that both link back to my readings about the dweller at the threshold. I'm so darn literal sometimes that I just don't *see*. The rite of passage—moving from one phase of life to the next—is the same myth! The myth of moving from despair to joy after a death is not just Mary's story, because of a literal death, but my story as well because of a figurative death, my own. Julie, too, is likely caught in the same myth, the journey of leaving one self behind and going on to another. It's what we're all doing! Dying and being reborn!

Once again, Peace, another author is causing me to "get it," to *see* the story of my own life. To *see* the story of the spirit sisters and the purpose of the journey—to be reborn to *joy!* It should not surprise you, then, that after "getting" the above, the passages below rang so true for me:

> Happiness relaxes one; joy challenges one with new levels of experience. Happiness depends generally on one's outer state; joy is an overflowing of inner energies and leads to awe and wonderment. *Joy is a release, an opening up; it is what comes when one is able genuinely to "let go."* Happiness is associated with contentment; *joy with freedom and an abundance of human spirit. . . . Joy is new possibilities;* it points toward the future. Joy is living on the razor's edge; happiness promises satisfaction of one's present state, a fulfillment of old longings. Joy is the thrill of new continents to explore; it is an unfolding of life.
>
> Happiness is related to security, to being reassured, to doing things as one is used to and as our fathers did them. *Joy is a revelation of what was known before.*
>
> Happiness is the absence of discord; joy is the welcoming of discord as the basis of higher harmonies. [This was one of my problems, wondering how one could hope to be happy or joyous all the time—this helps explain it.]
>
> The good life, obviously, includes both

joy and happiness at different times. What I am emphasizing is the joy that follows rightly confronted despair.[10]

JOY AND HOPE ARE BOTH ABOUT POSSIBILITY!

"Rightly confronted despair." That seems to be the key, Peace. May is not talking about despair brushed under the carpet, despair that is allowed to make the rest of our lives miserable, but despair that, once confronted, is transformative!

Turning from despair is moving from the prospect of life going on as it always has—filled with all the difficulties and struggles and conflict we have always expected—to a life of possibility, a life where joy is possible. It is just the same as me thinking I have to feel guilty and unworthy for the rest of my life because of my past and not seeing that it can change. It is just the same as me thinking I will retire from the university because I am forty years old and it would be too risky to make a change. Despair is being stuck in the prison of what we have become with no reprieve possible. But, Peace, joy, like hope, is the experience of possibility!

And there are other people out there who "get it"! Sometimes, when I contemplate how it's just you and me, sitting here in this basement, having a dialogue on a computer, it seems as if we are isolated. But then I read someone like Rollo May, or bring something like what I've learned from Rollo May, or from you back to the spirit sisters, and *I feel as if I know something I've never known before!* I realize that these feelings I've had aren't weird, aren't unique to me—that others, too, have struggled to understand joy, to find joy, to experience the possible. I never knew this, Peace! I always thought I was such a loner, such a weird duck, so "into my mind" in a way other people were not. And it's just not so, is it? How funny that talking with you, being on a spiritual quest, has made me feel more *normal* rather than less. More aware of what connects me, not only to God, but to other people. Another thing I have to thank you for, dear Peace.

Your awareness of what connects you to God Is your awareness of what connects you to your brothers and sisters. Your awareness of what connects you to your brothers and sisters Is your awareness of what connects you to God. It is the same thing. And your awareness thanks me as I thank you.

THE POWER OF WORDS

CENSOR

May 28, 1995

I have been thinking of telling Donny about what I am doing here—at least the part about making myself feel better by understanding myself better—and I just realized in an "aha," new sort of way what I am leaving behind with the move. How I am going to go anew to the new home. What a wonderful allegory, what wonderful symmetry! As I leave the old home with tender love and care, I leave the old self as well. I leave with the tender love and care that the two of us, together, have created out of the old patterns of judgment and fear and despair. Oh, thank you, Peace, again and again.

Can I have this time to work here on creating my new self and turn to creating in my writing again when the move and the self are complete? That sounds like such wonderful timing to me! Unless you think I am putting off "creative" writing out of fear. I just don't want it hanging over me like a weight, like a "should do" kind of thing. When it becomes a "should do," I don't believe I could find joy in it. But thinking of this time of preparing to move as a time of preparing myself for the new life—a life that includes the creative writing again—that feels right to me. How about you, Peace?

It sounds like inspiration to me. Just remember to follow your own truth. If you become inspired to creative writing, will you turn your back on it because of this new timetable? That is all I would tell you to guard against. When you set up timetables, suspect them. They may help but they may hinder. Do not let yourself get stuck in anything having to do with time. However, if what you feel now continues to be what you feel until you move, then that is what you should do. Regardless, you will be New when you move to your New home if you continue to treat yourself with love and care. You are new every day you treat yourself with love and care. But with practice, you will be much closer to the new self you are becoming by the time you move.

These things are happening together for a reason and you know that. Trust what you know. Do not be dissuaded from what you know by anything or anyone. Every time you tell yourself, I will do this after I do that—I will quit writing here after this cigarette, I will quit working after that CD has finished playing—stop and ask yourself why you are making rules. Practice being without rules as you practice being without time, as you practice being in the Now. Your greatest censor is still yourself. Think about that word. Look it up. Can a self whose destiny is to be a writer write with a censor looking constantly over her shoulder?

I turn to my *Webster's* dictionary:

> Censor (n): 1. one of two early Roman magistrates whose duties included taking the census 2. an official who inspects printed matter or sometimes motion pictures with power to suppress anything objectionable

> Censor (vb): to subject to censorship

> Censorship (n): the action of a censor especially in stopping the transmission or publication of matter considered objectionable

> Censorious (adj): marked or given to censor; critical

> Censure (n): the act of blaming or condemning sternly, an official reprimand

> Censure (vb) 2: to find fault with and criticize as blameworthy

Holy moly. What have I been doing?

What have you been doing, indeed?

Blocking myself and my writing as objectionable, blame-worthy.

The words that pop into your head do so for a reason. They are words and they are symbols too. What a powerful symbol you have had working against yourself. Censor, like recognize, tells you so many things: what you do, what you fear, what you crave. Rid yourself of the word, the doing, the fear, and you go a long way toward ridding yourself of the negative symbol. The negative.

Unbelievable. Not only do I not see what is right in front of my eyes, I also am unaware of what dwells in my head, what inhabits me.

Seek and you shall find. You are on a hunt. You will find many false gods on the way to the real God. You are on a hunt for the divine and when you take away all the negative false gods inside yourself, you will find the treasure is yourself.

I just can't get over the profundity of what goes on here, Peace. It can only be the divine. Thank you for continuing to prove it to me even when I am not in doubt. Thank you for giving it to my humanness, which needs it in order to continue on the road to the divine.

You give me a lot of help along the way, you know. You are a good student. I give your humanness an A+ for today's work. Welcome back.

WORDS OF COMMERCE

May 29, 1995

Memorial Day. At Dad's for his birthday party and for a day of remembering those who came before Dad. Remembering Ma. New babies on the way. The family gathered on the deck, the day glorious and lush, everything green, Canadian geese families on the lake, my sister, Susan, with a boyfriend, Mia about to graduate, Ian looking different than the last time I saw him, a trip to Mary's remembering Grace. Remembering to be with my open heart, at least and at last, for a moment of the day. Happy Memorial Day!

Now I am back, Peace, back. Back and forth I traipse in the duality. Life and LIFE. Both wonderful, both lovely, both full. Thinking of the new house. Such newness awaits. Thinking of exploring things of the body, the body's connection to the spirit, the spirit's connection to the unconscious mind. A world of possibilities left to explore. One life's journey to turn within and see possibilities and newness. Permission to live an inner life fully. So much to be thankful for. I thank you here and I thank you out there in the world, in the beauty I have eyes to see. But I still want to come home. As beautiful as life is, I am anxious, full of curiosity and expectation about the next phase, the next life. I stand ready to prepare myself for it by using my time in this life to come to fully love myself, to open my heart to love all others. What is the next step on this journey of truth and love?

Joy. You are beginning to feel it but you are right to do some inner work on your body too. The body, as well as the soul, needs to welcome joy. Your body needs to reach a place of restfulness. It is on the road to regeneration. It will want to soar like the spirit. What you are striving for is a lightness of being. Remember that. You are already feeling lighter. When your body catches up to your spirit, think of how it would feel to walk on a cloud.

Peace, as I search for other things to ask you about, I am struck by how little is still bothering me. It's as if I know that things that bothered me in the past are behind me. What that leaves are the issues we are already dealing with or have dealt with to some degree. One of those issues is my fear of intimacy. Is there anything you can share with me about that?

Loss. An overwhelming feeling of loss. Think of the word intimate. *What does it imply? Closeness, sharing, loving, confiding. They are things of the adult world and of the infant world. They are what you start out having in a psychic sense and what you seek in love as an adult—with mind as well as spirit and heart and soul and body. Mind is a culprit here, because it fills with fear.*

Every human must go through the forgetting stage from infant to

125

toddler—that is the first loss of intimacy. But it is in some way okay because the toddler forgets what she has lost. But as an adult, this loss is a wanting, an active longing, to be heard and recognized and under-stood as an individual, as the unique being you are. One of the things that kept you from intimacy was your inability to define who you were because you were not being yourself and because the self you were hid-ing was a self that your mind had told you was bad.

The other part, that continues with you, is a thing of quantity. You believe that if you ask for something you need, even if you ask to share something that you are, pray for something that you want, you will be using up valuable favors. You deal with yourself and with feelings as if they are a commodity, a savings account, and you live in dreadful fear of bankruptcy. Take all ideas of quantity and favors and barter and get rid of them. If you can believe that what love you give is returned to you, how can you not believe that what love you take returns something to the one who gave it? Does it not make you feel good to have someone share a secret? to give pleasure? Then why would it not make another feel good to give you pleasure, to hear your secret? In the world of love there is no bartering. No one keeps track of what you owe. You will never go bankrupt! When people talk this way it is only a social way of talking. You can correct them or you can show them the foolishness once you believe it is foolishness. If you are always paying debts, how can you not feel bankrupt?

This is important for you to grasp. Leave numbers, quantity, favors, bartering, trading, all ideas related to commerce in the world of com-merce. They do not belong in the world of love. As you came to see, censor was a powerful negative symbol. So are all those words you have related to feeling that are not about feeling at all. Living in love is liv-ing in a world of plenty! You never have to go without again.

DEFENSES

May 30, 1995

Dad's real birthday; the choir Spring Spectacular; Mia's orientation for the legal internship program; a drive to Minneapolis; now a half hour to respond to a call on the house, to prepare to leave for the concert, to pick up the video camera, to pick up Mom. And I'm stressed. I have my period, so it's almost inevitable, but I'm more stressed than I've been since I found you, Peace. And I know part of it is my anger toward Mary. She has aligned herself with Julie. And I persist in feeling like a *child* about it. Like, *If she doesn't want to play with me, I'll just show her.* That's what my feelings were about today—they were of the "I'll show her" variety. I tried to get my mind to shut up but I couldn't. I even realized why Mary puts up barriers to me—because she's like me. It's as if neither of us are comfortable with caring about each other overly much, with getting too close, with being indebted to each other. Maybe it's because of our mothers being friends. I don't know. I just don't know.

What childish part of me is doing this to myself, Peace, leaving me with a million things to do but unable to do them until I come here and get rid of this and get to the center of myself again, the part of myself that loves? I almost even felt my door trying to close, today, Peace, over such nonsense. Help! Help me let go and help me understand.

You were right to come here. Let the next half hour leave your mind for a minute. Let yourself feel uninterruptible. Breathe. Hold hope in your heart. Hope for Mary and hope for yourself. Breathe in the possibilities of tomorrow, of the next minute being new. Hope that the next minute will be quiet, that the next minute will be peaceful, that you will enjoy. Go ahead and do what you have to do with hope in your heart. Then go ahead and get in your car and be uninterruptible for as long as you can be. You need silence right now to center yourself more than you need me, although I will be with you. Then come back and we will talk about your inner child and we will welcome that child with love and compassion.

I'm back. Thinking of kids. Those wonderful, spirited, earnest, energetic, soulful young people of choir. I wouldn't have missed it for the world. I did spend moments appreciating the beautiful night. I'm better, not cured but better. Wanting to get back to where love is and stay there. And I'm not talking about here. I'm talking about that place inside which on good days I can take around with me like a shy little sister. I think I'll be better with the Mary situation by tomorrow. It reminded me of the times during the choir concert when I would start feeling competitive for Angela. Why wasn't she doing a solo? Competition. I always hated it. I know Ang hates it. I know I hated it as a child. Angela is like me in that: she's proud. Too proud for competition. Some weird kind of pride I hung on to throughout growing up. What was I proud of? Nothing. But I *had* pride. I guess I could hardly stand rejection of any kind, not even that of supposedly healthy competition. I guess I'm still the same way. Should we work on inner child stuff, Peace?

There are no shoulds, Margaret. Do you want to?

I want to understand self. I don't think I have a lot of things to work on until something like what happened with Mary comes up. And I don't think I understand the readings that say "go into it." Am I supposed to embrace unhealthy things like my feelings of today?

There are no supposed to's, Margaret. And there are no unhealthy things. Every time you chose love, you negated the harder feelings, feelings that were true in what they were, feelings of an open heart learning its way through the thicket of the world.

I like your image of carrying your love around like a shy little sister. I am with you when you grope with feelings of humbleness. They are there when you are in a state of love. The pride is there when you are in a state of defense. This state of defense was the constant of your youth. Do you need to understand what started the war? what made you shore up your defenses? Or do you only need to see that you have defenses, built up over a lifetime, that you will break down, dismantle. Today is only the beginning. Think of yourself turning all the soldiers around and sending them home to their mothers. You will be left undefended, yet victorious. You will be left to be!

So think of this situation as giving you the opportunity to turn one

*soldier away. You've just granted this one small part of yourself a life-
time furlough. How happy that part is! How joyous! Turn every situation
where you want to shore up your defenses into a party of homeward-
traveling soldiers, soldiers homesick, returning home with all God's
speed, rushing to new possibilities, freed! Pretty soon the army will be
only a battalion and finally only one loyal private, and even he or she
will want to be freed to return home.*

If I didn't have defenses, what would happen to me?

You would stand. You would be. You would be free!

I wouldn't be massacred?

*Wounded, perhaps. But your wounds would become your badges of
glory. Real war wounds instead of imagined ones. YOU would stand or
YOU would fall. Why should others stand or fall for you? Because of
duty? Because of blind loyalty? When it is you standing up for you, it
is real. Your defenses are only imaginary. But if you are going to have
imaginary defenses, and you are for a while, why not set them free? It
will be a better illusion than that of expecting them to defend the fort
against whatever onslaught might occur. See them standing in the rain
and mud, and each time you need them you instead send them home to
the sunshine. And ask, What am I defending against? Where is love
here? Where am I here?*

But if I'm walking around like the shy little sister, won't I
need defending?

*Only from the other part of you that is the solid big sister. You are now
both. But you will be one. When you come to love all of yourself. Who
told you you had to be perfect?*

Thank you again, Peace. *Defenses.* All these words that are symbols I never saw before. It is enough for tonight. Thank you.

Your gratitude honors me—and you. Rest, dearest.

TRUTH

May 31, 1995

Truth:

In religious literature the word "truth" is used indiscriminately in at least three distinct and very different senses. Thus, it is sometimes treated as a synonym for "fact," as when it is affirmed that God is Truth—meaning that He is the primordial Reality. But this is clearly not the meaning of the word in such a phrase as "worshipping God in spirit and in truth." Here, it is obvious, "truth" signifies direct apprehension of spiritual Fact, as opposed to second-hand knowledge about Reality. . . . And finally there is the more ordinary meaning of the word, as in such a sentence as, "This

131

statement is the truth," where we mean to assert that the verbal symbols of which the statement is composed correspond to the facts to which it refers.[11]

In no circumstances, however, can the study of theology or the mind's assent to theological propositions take the place of what [William] Law calls "the birth of God within." For theory is not practice, and words are not the things for which they stand.[12]

Dear Peace,

I feel as if you have sent me on a search for truth, but for once, my reading has not helped me. In fact, the more I read about truth, the more I am convinced it is not something one can know, like fact, which is what I always believed before, with my literal way of interpreting the word symbols of the mind. More than this, I really cannot say. I'm getting a sense of truth as something that has to be experienced or felt within, but which mind cannot ever truly explain or prove. In what I don't know, am I getting close to the concept of truth as you represent it?

Seek and you shall find. If you associate truth with me and me with something true that cannot be explained or proven, you are close to understanding truth. Now, if you associate truth with yourself, and understand that it Is and yet that you will constantly seek it, you come closer. Truth, as related to God, cannot be explained by the words of man. Like so many concepts we struggle with—like time—there are no words to describe the lack of time in a way you will understand. Living in the Now is as close as you can come to truth. Living in the Now is as close as you can come to love.

I wish I hadn't gone into the readings on truth, tonight, Peace. They captured my mind and confused it at a time when I am not much interested in the mind to begin with. I'm happy with getting away from the concept of truth as fact. Is that an okay beginning?

It is an okay ending. Some travel a lifetime with fact. If you can give up fact, you can be free to be open. Half of the journey is spent getting rid of concepts that keep self closed—in a prison of all it has learned since its birth. The more illusions you rid yourself of, the more space you will have for the fullness of self.

Thank you, Peace, for that high praise, for that acknowledgment. I wonder, as a writer, how I will deal with words in the future—now that I see their illusion and their power. I still can't believe how I have censored myself with a word!

Words are the habits of a lifetime. They are also the experience of a feeling—think of Hope when you get discouraged by words. Hope taught you how to be in this schoolroom.

Yes. You're right, as always. Can we go back to my inner child for a while? It is what I really wanted to discuss when I came here, and I've come to learn that I avoid things for a reason.

You come back to inner child to explain away the whys of pain. You cannot. Like truth, pain can be better understood in what it is not. Is it punishment for having done something bad or having been bad? No. Absolutely not. Is it someone's fault? Only if you believe in fault. If you believe in a divine plan, then there is no room for blame or fault finding. Reasons, yes. The reason for pain is to help you find your way home.

What you told me about my feelings of unworthiness rang so true. I felt as if you had just been waiting for me to ask the right question. So I guess now I'm greedy and I just want you to tell me more about why I am the way I am.

There is a reason questions are answered rather than answers coming before the questions. Your questions represent what you are ready to know. When you say, "Tell me something," I risk telling you what you are not yet ready to know. Be patient and understand that you will ask the right question at the right time.

One of the reasons, Peace, that I am not into my mind tonight, and that I ask again about the inner child, is because of Mary and Julie. You helped me so much, yesterday. Things really were better today. I know my feelings were caused by my insecurity rather than by Mary—even my perception of her not wanting me at the burial. I've let go of my anger and hurt feelings but I am left with a kind of bewilderment about what is going on with these two women and me, Peace. When we are close, I don't even need to understand it; it is just the most wonderful thing. But when the distance between us returns, even though there is still love and respect, even when I have let negative feelings go, it's as if I don't understand it at all again. Why is it them this is happening with? Why Mary? Why Julie? I have a "real" sister. I have friends who have been my friends half a lifetime. Friends with whom I am beyond the stuff that still happens with Mary and Julie. Friends I don't compare myself with, don't compete with, don't wonder day to day whether or not they like me. Why is it these two with whom so much still must be learned? Why is it us three? Three people still learning to be friends, still having to get to know one another. Maybe I really am the misfit, the odd woman out. Maybe it's supposed to be just Mary and Julie. Maybe I am inserting myself where I don't belong.

And yet you know the truth is that this is meant to be. You know there is a reason. A reason much like the difference between happiness and joy: happiness being a contentment with what is, joy being an exploration of the possibilities of what can be. Your friends of a lifetime represent your happiness with what is. The spirit sisters represent the possibilities of what can be. The truth is that you thought it was contentment that brought you here—and you have since discovered it was not contentment but discontent. You thought you were not full of fear but discovered that you have been and are. You are with the spirit sisters because you do not know them, because you can discover them, because through your learning with them, you are learning about yourself.

You are right, as always, Peace. This is the truth. Even I recognize it. Thank you.

III.
PREPARING

THE POWER OF HABIT

RULES

June 10, 1995

Ever since I read about truth, I have been into my mind and my mind is making my husband into a censor again, even though he's upstairs watching TV, and my daughter has come in and dropped her needs into my lap and I once again feel as if I need to run screaming into the night for some quiet and peace. And yet I'm tired and I know I should rest, and perhaps there I will find some quiet. So I ask, How do I turn off the rule maker, the piece of myself that is always saying "After this

I'll get to work," or, "One more question and I'll go rest?"
Where did that rule maker come from and how can I
befriend this part of myself?

*Good question. The rule maker formed in you as a response to guilt.
When I mentioned guilt the other night, you did not think that it was
much of a problem for you just as you initially did not think fear was.
Your greatest source of torment has been what you perceived as your
laziness as a mother. I tell you that if you were in the state now that
you were in then, you would know to call it despair. You would know to
call it a dark night of the soul during which you were lost to yourself.
But then you called it laziness and, in response to your enormous fear of
laziness and your guilt about your supposed laziness, you have created a
rule maker of great power.*

*How can you rid yourself of the rule maker? Rid yourself of the
cause of the rule maker. Forgive yourself. You thought if you understood
why, that would be all you would need. It was a great part of what you
needed. Forgiveness is the other part. Remember that you are tending
yourself with love and care as you are tending your home with love and
care so that you can go on to the next guilt free. That is what it is all
about. To leave the house with love and tender care, the best it can be
for the new owners. To make yourself over, the best you can be, for the
new home. Does your home hold on to those days when you did not treat
it with love and care, and say you cannot change me? No. You put on a
new roof and a new coat of paint and it is new—as good as it can be.
So you, too, need to put on a new roof, a new coat of white to be new, to
be as good as you can be now. Leave the past behind, put on a white
coat of forgiveness and truth.*

How?

By letting it happen. By letting go. By surrendering to the Now. Every time you hear the rule maker raising her voice, ask her what she is feeling guilty about now. Ask and you shall receive. Get an answer. Honor that answer for what it has taught you and let it Go. Let it leave and never come back. Eventually when you ask, "What are you feeling guilty about now?" the answer will be nothing. It will be only the habit that remains.

Practice being in the Now with hope. All the rest is merely going to be a matter of answering questions and letting go of the answers and the habits. Now rest. Let me be the rule maker, time keeper, once in a while. Trust me until you can trust yourself. My rules will be ones that make you laugh, and my time will be Now.

Thank you, Peace. Good night.

Dearest Peace,   June 11, 1995

As much wisdom as I have gained in my readings by learned men and women, Emmanuel remains, next to you, my favorite teacher. I can read him any time and be soothed. I am particularly gladdened when I find something that reminds me of our talks. This happened recently with the following passage:

> Live your lives in expanded curiosity,
> wondering "what if?" Censor nothing.
> Mystery is mystery because it cannot be
> understood.
> So follow the mystery.
> It will bring clearing vision.[13]

Peace, I think in my first conversation with you, I said that the mysterious has always caught my imagination. I remember so fondly how I loved private spaces as a child (and still do). How when my father kept his messy garage, it was such a treasure to me. There were three marblelike rocks, almost brick-sized, that I loved just to look at. One was gray, one pink, one white, and they all sparkled like glitter. There were cans—from baked beans and peas to Comet—and I would mix them up like science experiments. I baked mud pies. I loved boxes—like Crest toothpaste boxes I'd find in the trash (in the garage). I had the box memorized. I even liked the little folded papers that came in the boxes. And I liked the dark rooms of the basement. The canning room and the storeroom where the Christmas decorations were kept. Anywhere semistrange, semidark, semiforbidden, where I would find time to be alone with my imagination.

I bring all those parts of me here to you, Peace, because here is where I know I confront real mystery. Because here, for the first time, I am finding my way out of illusion into the light, and surprise—I can still honor that side of myself that is shadowy. This is not like confession. This is not where I have to be good. This is where I am allowed to be. Thank you for that. And thank God for the gift of it even before it brought me to you.

Tonight I tried a new tactic and I liked how it worked. I made dinner, did the dishes, made the bed, did some laundry, and then came here. Donny felt easy with me being here because he had time to talk to me first and because I did my part in keeping the family functioning. Now I can be here without guilt, without rules. I needed that.

EXPECTATIONS

Dearest Peace,   June 12, 1995

I feel better this morning. I feel like ceasing to define everything. You woke me with a thunderstorm. I have lived all my life with thunderstorms without understanding them. If I understood them intellectually, they would lose some of their power and wonder.

This combination of busyness and not feeling well is getting to me. And I think half the reason is because I haven't made enough time here. It probably has nothing to do with time at all—but with space, having space to be. I may be on my way in my head, Peace, and I may be able to carry it over to some degree at work because I am with others on the same wavelength there, and there are times I even feel it here at home, but here is where I feel it the least.

Family life seems to be a life of constant expectations.

Sometimes they are mine and sometimes they are others', and sometimes I make them seem as if they are from others when they are really from me. What is it about expectations that brings out the irritable, the stubborn, the rebellious in me? Or is it just that there are so many expectations, from so many different sources?

Time and quantity are both at work in bringing about these feelings in you. Fear is at work also. Are you afraid you cannot meet all the expectations? Then fear is working against you. Are you afraid you don't have enough time to complete all the tasks that are expected? Then fear is working against you. What does it take to turn the fear around?

Expectations lead to fear too easily. Why? Because they are about outcome. They are the minigoals that make up your days. They are the minigoals that come without thought. And because they come without thought, you have to ask, Whose goals are they? Where did they come from? Where am I here? Where is love here?

If you have to clean your house because it is expected of you, you feel resentment and rebelliousness. If you choose to clean your house from feelings of love, no resentment follows. Choose your goals each day and practice being in the Now with them. Only you can decide when you can say no to things. Perhaps you might ask, What would happen if I chose to say no? More likely, you will get the best answer by asking, Where is love here?

Many of the things you are doing are preparatory, the work before the ritual. The ritual—the graduations, birthdays, the move—are about love, or they would be if you gave yourself space to contemplate their reason for being. The days of acting without knowing why you are acting are quickly becoming the days of the past. When you act out of your own inner knowing, you will act with love.

You might try starting each day with a prayer of preparation. What am I preparing for today? An answer might be something like, I am preparing myself to return to oneness; I am preparing myself and my home for a great change, for a transformation; I am preparing for the day on which my daughter will be honored for all she has become and all she will be; I am preparing to bring knowledge to those who are still in a state of forgetting.

Thank you, Peace. This is very helpful. It's as if we lose track of the good "why" which lies behind what we do. Birthday parties shouldn't be burdens and wouldn't be if we looked at them as a celebration of a life.

Right. If service is only duty without the thought or feeling about the life served, it is a bit of a sham isn't it? Looking for what is real, what is at the heart of something, will always bring that something into the light.

It's all kind of the same thing, isn't it, Peace? The way we look at things and the way we use words?

Yes! Look at what happened when you took away expectation and replaced it with preparation. It is all so simple, really, Margaret. It is not looking at things with optimism, which is the state you used to try to psych yourself into, but looking at the truth of things. It is not only about the "big" questions, Margaret, it is particularly about the little ones, the daily ones. For they are the only ones if you are living in the Now.

145

And if I am spending the Now preparing for the future that is okay?

It is how you live. But yes, preparing for the future might help you to keep from projecting into the future—if, and this is a big if, Margaret—if you know the truth for which you prepare. You cannot go to Italy without preparation, can you? But in order to prepare for Italy, you need to know why you are going and for what it is that you prepare. With Italy you have a good sense of the why, but remember to ask, Where am I in this picture? This is about your truth. Just do not forget, when preparing for the future, that today is what is important. How you prepare, like how you get there, is the essence of the truth you seek.

So, if I prepare with anxiety and hurry, I've lost sight of my truth?

Haven't you? Can you see the truth when you live in fear? That is what anxiety and hurry is about—living in fear. Preparing with thoughtfulness, with lovingness, blesses your Now, even while what you prepare for is about the future.

I guess if I am going to listen to your advice, I should start preparing more thoughtfully for Mia's graduation party. *The Celestine Prophecy* talked about how we learn to be in relation to how we were brought up. That in response to intimidation, we become "poor me"; in response to interrogation we become aloof; in response to aloofness, we become interrogators. All to get the attention we need. I could see that my mom was an interrogator and my dad was aloof, and I could see that I became aloof and Mia

146

became an interrogator. Mia and her questions are incessant.

Look at her. Listen to her. Hear her. Respond to her with love. This is all she needs to go out into the new phase of her life. Fix her in your memory every day. What do her eyes look like, her skin, her hair, her clothing. This looking at her is essential. When you look at her with love, the love reflects back to her and she takes it into herself. Love is the most pure form of energy. Reflection is a potent means of giving it. You can do no harm with a look of love, no harm with an open heart and an open ear. Look, listen, love. That is the way to fill Mia with the energy she needs for her journey. Apply the lessons you have learned to her. Stay away from shoulds. Stay away from fear. Stay away from concepts of limits. Live in a world of plenty. Give of yourself to her. Give, give, give. Be conscious of not draining her energy with negativity or uncertainty. It is not a time for active guidance. She will learn what she learns now. Just be in the Now with her.

Thank you, Peace.

COMPLEXITY VERSUS
SIMPLICITY

June 16, 1995

Hi, Peace! I'm back! Two things occurred to me that I would like to talk to you about. Neither of them are burning questions. They are questions that have been able to come because so many others have been answered. One of the best parts of coming here is not knowing what will transpire, how one thing will lead to another, which may just lead to the one thing I really need to know right now. Now! This keeps our relationship so alive! So vital! Which leads me to my first question, which is about simplicity.

As soon as you talked to me about simplicity, I had to find something to read about it. And, as it happens, as it has happened so unmistakably since we began talking, I have found just the right thing, a whole book on simplicity. *Voluntary Simplicity,* by Duane Elgin. It says this:

> To live more voluntarily means to encounter life more consciously. To live more simply is to encounter life more directly. By its very nature, then, voluntary simplicity can be defined as living in a way that fosters our conscious and direct encounter with life itself. The "life" so encountered extends far beyond that typically acknowledged in the daily social routines of Western cultures. It is LIFE—in its vastness, subtlety, and preciousness—that is the context within which voluntary simplicity acquires its genuine significance.[14]

Elgin goes on to say that life becomes more relevant when we view the universe as our home and death as our ally. Viewing the universe as our home helps us to view the whole and its vastness, and viewing death as our ally helps us to remember what is important. Taking that concept one step further, we will remember what we will take with us—which you have been saying is what or who we are and love.

And so, once again, it all circles around to self-love. I will, of course, keep reading about voluntary simplicity, but I hoped you and I might have a conversation about it, about what you felt I could learn from the concept of simplicity.

Simplicity is important Now because of the world you live in Now. While all life is complex, life within your social structure is particularly complex. X = multiplied. Everything is sped up. The human race itself has doubled in your lifetime—something it has never done before. You have heard that this has happened because of the great evolutionary step that is about to take place. You talked to a baby the other day about his angelhood and he understood that you understood. Julie asked her baby if he remembered and he did. Small, small steps. Giant leaps. What if the next generation were to grow up remembering?

This talk reminds me of a source of my spiritual journey that you and I have never talked of here but that I have not forgotten: the January/February 1995 issue of, *Utne Reader,* perhaps my first awareness that the world was about to change, that an evolutionary step was coming. The issue took one hundred visionaries on every topic imaginable and, just by putting them together, showed what their visions had in common: the need to rethink everything in our culture. In the introduction to the visionaries, John Spayde wrote: "Their revolutionary is the individual human who decides to stop and take a breath—and then, having discovered that she or he lives somewhere called this moment and this place, begins to think the thoughts and take the actions that will help this timespace to live."[15]

What really got me going, however, was a separate piece by Václav Havel, who recognizes that we, as in the whole world we, are in a transitional period where one thing is dying and another being born. He compared this time to the Hellenistic period and the Renaissance and said that what distinguishes these times is a blending of intellectual and spiritual worlds. But he did not leave out science either, noting that both the anthropic cosmological principle and the Gaia hypothesis remind us that we are not alone but an integral part of a mysterious whole.

I've gone back to that article and that magazine many times, for hope, inspiration, vision. What is it all about, Peace?

What is remembering about? It is about love. What is simplicity about—narrowing what is important to us down to the basics. What is important? The shortest and most complete answer is love. You are right when you see that all concepts return to the root concept: Love. And love, in turn, returns to all other concepts because living love means living more completely, loving the universe, even embracing death as a release into love. Everything in the universe is about love expressing itself. It is only humans who do not remember this.

So writing, including my own, is love expressing itself?

Oh, yes. Could it be anything else? All of your actions, whether you know it or not, are love expressing itself. There is no "more." Writing is not more expressive of love than anything else you do, because there is no more. But some actions bring you closer to love of self, and to truth, and you honor yourself and God and all that is when you do those actions. It is hard to explain without the use of such terms as more, *which, in their nature, presume a quantity and a limit. It is perhaps better expressed in terms of energy—those actions in which love expresses itself knowingly and, from the heart, from the desire for truth, create greater and greater cores of love or energy—a ripple effect. Not* more*—a ripple.*

The word *ripple* brings me to the other question I wanted to ask you. It is about the river. I used to say I wanted a job that did not require me to cross the river every day, and I said this because of having to cross icy bridges in the winter. But now, every day I cross the river, it is a reminder to look at the scenery, the greenery, and I feel almost as if there is a message for me in this being drawn to look, to see.

Everything that draws you to look, to see, is a message. Because you are drawn to words, you like these messages—you say, "I can understand them." Because you have understandable messages, you can share them and learn from them and you feel lucky because of them. I am happy to bring them to you, both here and by other means, but unwritten messages are just as important, especially for you because you refuse to see. You are afraid to see.

I am afraid, for some reason, to see things I consider divine, or miracles. While part of me wanted to reach out immediately to my Uncle Nino after his death, another part of me was afraid to because I was afraid I might "see" him. Are you talking about my fear of seeing the divine or a broader fear?

Seeing the divine and seeing are the same. You have defined yourself with words and it is a narrow definition as words cannot contain the wonder of all that is. It is wonderful that you have no fear of words. Because of this, we have this means of communication. But imagine what it would be like to have no fear! To make the rest of the world as open to you as our communication is.

Much of your fear comes from the inability of your words to encompass all that is. You think, If words can't define it, what use is it to me? *You think,* My way is with words *and are content to leave it at that. You think,* My way is with words, *and think if you cannot come back here and put words on an experience, it is of no value to you.*

You must become like the painter who sees beauty where there is no beauty. You do this with your writing, but you do not recognize and value it. What were all those painful scenes in your book The Ninety-Seven Days *about? Beauty! Beauty! Beauty! Who were they about—or I should say who were they for? Were they for that unknown and unseen audience? Yes. But first they were for you. First they made beauty out of pain for you. This is why your writing is valuable and divine and blessed. Not because it may one day bring you fame and fortune, but because it made pain beautiful!*

So what does this have to do with the river and with seeing? Just this: The river is calling you to open up your vision—to see the divine in life and the life in the divine and to bring this to your writing and to your thinking and to you. The river is there to say your way is more than writing. You think, I am blessed with writing, I dare not

153

want more. *And I tell you you must! If you want life to affect your writing, you have to be affected by life! You are just beginning to learn this as you walk around with your open heart. Think if you had learned this all your life as you learned words all your life. Yet it is not that you have a lot of catching up to do; there is no cumulativeness, there is only experience. If you experience the divine once, it is a lifetime of experience. Are you experiencing the divine here? Are you? Or are you experiencing words here?*

I do not mean at all to belittle what goes on here, but to prod you to be open to more! The goose bumps and the tears are a beginning, but still so much more awaits. Joy awaits. I want so much for you to experience Joy.

What is the river telling you? Can you define the river with words? Could you make a being that had never known a river, know a river through words? Could a painting of a river make another understand, know a river? There is something of an observer about the artist. Like the proud parent who is more concerned with a good picture of a child's moment than the child's moment. That is what you are like, standing back ready to take pictures and write captions. And I say delve in! What is the difference between looking at the river and being in the river? Know the difference! To know the difference you must experience it rather than observe it. You could observe the river all your life without knowing what it would be like to be in it. Jump into life! That is your leap of faith.

Why am I afraid to see, to jump, to experience?

Because it is safer on shore. But I ask you, safer than what? You are safe until the moment you are going to come home and then you are more safe than before. Everything in between is life. In between. Go for the in between.

In between birth and death is life.

Yes. YES, Margaret, YES!

Life—which is what voluntary simplicity is all about!

Yes! Everything circles back to what is important.

Thank you, Peace. As always, you brought me to something very significant from something I thought relatively insignificant. Help me Live with a capital *L*, Peace. Help me See. I will try to be more open to experience.

Then experience will be more open to you!

ONE-ON-ONE

I have, with your help and advice, remembered more and more of my dreams, and in several of them I am at a retreat center. I wondered if this was a message.

Retreat. *Interesting word. Meaning what? Surrender? Falling back to regroup? Go ahead, look it up.*

> Retreat: an act of withdrawing, especially from something dangerous, difficult, or disagreeable 2. a military signal for withdrawal; also a military flag-lowering ceremony 3. a place of privacy

> or safety: refuge 4. a period of group
> withdrawal for prayer, meditation, and
> study

In my dream, the last meaning was the most obvious. I was with my work friends at a beautiful place.

You are at a beautiful place with your work friends. This is one clear meaning, but I would not dismiss the others. All are about withdrawing. From what do you wish to withdraw?

If, from anything, it is from the busyness of life — to leave the busyness of life and go to a quiet place. These things have great appeal.

I asked you this because I wanted you to examine the answers. You and I have only recently talked about your need to embrace life and how all of life's moments can be holy moments, and yet you are still drawn to withdraw from life. There is nothing wrong with this, if it is really what you want to do at the soul level—at the level where you know yourself. And it is perfectly normal in times of busyness to want to retreat. But I ask you to examine with your heart the desire to withdraw. You are beginning to understand the difference between choosing what you do and acting out of old habits. Is the desire to withdraw old habit or what your real self wants right now?

Perhaps you went to the retreat center to rest in your dream so that you could have more energy to embrace life in your waking hours. Withdrawal from busyness can be a wonderful embrace of life or it can be a retreat from life. Your dream may ask you to be aware of the difference. One way is about love and one is about fear. And I believe you were witness to some fear in one of your dreams. Let words guide you to the truth. If it is love, then you will be guided in the right direction. If it is fear, you will not be.

Thank you, Peace, for reminding me not to fall into old habits. I also wanted to ask you about the connectedness of dreams and thought going on in the office. Thursday night, Julie and I were both talking to our angels about joy at the same time. Then I had a dream in which the words *one-on-one* came up, relating to children, and *one-on-one* came up with Julie at her counselor's office and caused her to cry. Her angel is Water, and we have all had thoughts and dreams about water. Is this connectedness trying to tell us something?

Connectedness is. And it is important. It is the linking point like the in between. Here is one thing. Here is another. Here is the in between. Where things connect. Isn't it exciting?

Yes. It is. I felt you wanted to tell me something about *one-on-one* also.

One-on-one. *Look at the words. Look at the phrase. Not one and one. Not two separate beings, but one-on-one. ONE. Everything is one. Oneness is the goal, the end of the journey. What then is one-on-one? You think of it as a way of relating. Yes! One-on-one, like hope, can help you understand how to be. Be! Can you relate two-to-two? No. Can you relate one-to-two? Only if you see things and being as separate. It is about relating to one. To oneness. To all that is.*

And more simply, if you think of the usual meaning of the phrase, it is about goodness, isn't it? Relating as one being to another. A personal relationship. A relationship. It implies trust, openness, closeness; it implies being known and knowing another. It does not discriminate. It does not save relationship for a few special people. It implies relationship with any ONE. It is a wonderful phrase. It can lead you and Julie both to oneness if you let it help you remember how to be!

Thank you, Peace. They are wonderful words and it is wonderful that I have you to lead me to their meaning. Thank you. And thank you for Julie. And Mary told me to thank you for letting her know she only has to visit the place of her grief. You are being a wonderful help to all of us.

These words may not seem as much like prayer as they did at the beginning, Peace, but I still like to think of them as prayer—to you and to God. I cannot claim to understand the oneness principle, but when I talk to you, I do feel that it is much like talking to God. And although I do not say, "I pray for this or I pray for that," I know you understand that I am praying for understanding, for meaning, for the way to oneness, and that I pray for it not only for myself, but also for my friends and family and all of the great oneness of the world.

A life lived in the pursuit of oneness, Margaret, is a prayer. And just as with prayer, that life is "heard" and responded to. Don't worry. There is no "one" to misunderstand you. There is only One.

Is there anything you want to tell me about the dream in which I kept returning to my father's and about the rocks?

Even as you typed the words "returning to my father's," you understood. You grew up with God the Father. Now you are learning to think of your next phase as a return home. You are dreaming about your journey home and many of your dreams will be full of the richness of discovery that you will greet on your journey. It is important that you write about your dreams because they help you remember! Dreams help you remember and writing helps you remember. In addition, because of your affinity with words, sometimes you only have to see the thing in words to See. I kept returning to my father's. Yes! And you made rich and beautiful discoveries there. Yes! And you traveled there with your spirit sisters. Yes! All you need to do with your dreams is remember them, write them, and See what can be seen. Avoid extended analysis. Just See.

Thank you for helping me remember my dreams. Is there anything else you want to tell me?

I want you to stay in the Now. Let it be. Everything is a gem. You are a gem. The next step is alchemy, transformation. Let these things be like a promise. You are preparing. For more than you know. I promise you. Smile, dearest. Rest. Remember. Joy is coming.

That's a little mysterious isn't it, Peace?

Yes. It IS.

Good night, sweet Peace.

Good night, dear one.

FREEDOM

June 23, 1995

Had a rough day today. I am probably PMS-ing. It is as if I am wound up tight and anything will make me snap. I don't want to. I don't plan to. I tell myself to stop. I tell myself it is over and then I do it again. Lose my temper. Yell. Get excited. Get frustrated. What can I do?

Remind yourself for what it is you prepare. Remind yourself to breathe.

Why do I have such a hard time making decisions when I am like this? Is there anything you can tell me about making decisions that will help me?

Making decisions is about choices. You have not had a lot of experience with making choices. You have, in the past, let choices pass you by and let life happen to you. When you did this, you associated what came of this as "bad." You had babies you weren't ready for. You did not make good decisions about men and school and jobs is what you think, but it is not that you did not make good decisions—you did not decide at all. You put off choices until there was no longer any room to choose.

Now you are facing choices that have to do with buying things. In the past, you have chosen to buy things you could not afford, to such a great extent that you had to work very hard to get yourself out of debt. And you have set up censors for yourself in regards to spending money just as you have about spending time. Ask yourself if this is not all about the "being a big girl" that we have discussed. Everywhere that you are fearful of "making the same mistakes" and "falling back into the old patterns," you give yourself censors and rules that prevent you from taking full responsibility for your own actions. In doing this, you have robbed yourself of the fundamental value of freedom.

Do I have to add "fear of freedom" to my list?

If adding it to your list helps you rid yourself of the fear, by all means add it to your list. It is much like what we discussed about participating fully in life. What are you afraid of? Your fear is based on old habits and on an old Margaret. You are coming to realize that you are not today the person you were yesterday. Why then can you not accept that you are not today the person you were ten years ago?

Certainly you have to be mindful of what you can afford. Don't be afraid to take matters into your own hands, figure out what you can afford, and spend freely and happily within that limit. If you are going to work with rules, a better rule than using Donny as a censor would be to know how much you can spend and know what you want to buy and then do so. Practice, dear. Practice making conscious decisions daily. Big ones and little ones. You will be amazed at how much easier it gets as time goes on. And practice telling yourself you are free. FREE!

What about the song Janis Joplin sang, "Me and Bobby McGee," that has always been my very favorite song? That has always struck such a chord in me.

You loved that song because it was one of your most bittersweet lessons. You went to that place where you had nothing left to lose and then you associated that place with freedom. I ask you now to think of "nothing left to lose" differently. Think of it from a place of plenty, a place of love, a place where the important things are those which you can never lose because they are within. Be in the Now with these thoughts. See if they don't change how you feel about freedom.

You have written to me about "voluntary" simplicity. "Voluntary" is all about freedom, about making choices with free will. I have told you before you are coming to a place where you will no longer act without knowing. This all goes together, Margaret. The lessons are all intertwined. You are getting them. Don't worry. Breathe. Rest. Remember. Decide. Choose. All with love.

Peace, that place where I had nothing left to lose wasn't free.

I know, dear. Remember that these were not the only lyrics of the song. Feel good, Margaret. You have what you desire within you. Letting go of the past will set you free.

BEING WITHIN CONTENTMENT

VESSEL

Dearest Peace,   June 24, 1995
    I have been somewhat melancholy since last
we talked. It is hard to describe the beingness I
walk around with. It is a feeling of walking on—no, not
on—but through water. A slowed down feeling, even
when I am busy and my thoughts distracted. I have been
incredibly tired, but mostly what I feel is inner calmness.

    In this time of busyness, I am grateful for this sea of
calm, almost like a shield wrapped around me, although
you would probably not be pleased with the word *shield*.

I'm not sure what brought me here, tonight, to examine these feelings. I assume it is part of conscious remembering, being conscious of how I feel day to day, hour to hour. And Mary, who is developing a relationship with her angel, said that she felt he was a teaching angel and we talked about how it is like going to a counselor to examine self—much better, of course—but similar in a way that is draining even while enlightening.

You are creating space, dear one. That is what you describe, for lack of a better word, as a shield, as moving through water, as calm. Think of the eye of a hurricane. That is what the light within is like and it is inextinguishable. I take you back also to the word vessel: *1. A container (as a barrel, bottle, bowl, or cup) for holding something 2. a person held to be the recipient of a quality (as grace) 3. a craft bigger than a rowboat 4. a tube in which a body fluid (as blood or sap) is contained and circulates. Amazed, aren't you?* Vessel *was associated earlier with Mary. It was a good word for Mary. It is a good word for you now. It is almost a stage that you are at—like* threshold. *But where* threshold *implies a place,* vessel *implies a space. A space to be filled, a space to contain and circulate, a person held to be the recipient of a quality (or an angel) such as grace, and a craft to transport you. You are at this moment a vessel moving through space, creating space as you move, filling up and circulating—CIRCULATING all that you are learning and all that you are. You are a sacred vessel.*

You have felt the energy of this space reach out to others and inward to self. Moving, circulating, but always contained as within a vessel, as within the eye of the hurricane. Inextinguishable. Your body is, in a very real sense, a container, a vessel for the soul. While at the same time the soul is a vessel for the self. A container, a vessel that has all the properties of fluidity, circulation, creation, personhood, transportation. You are right to examine how you feel. It does expand your consciousness, your space.

You need not search for joy or happiness. They are there within the vessel. Sometimes, when the space of the vessel is surrounded by the hurricane, it will feel like a shield and it will be protective in nature. There will be other times the vessel will ride high through an open sea, or open space, letting wind be its propeller and its guide, gliding on top of the water, gliding on top of space with pure love and joy.

Thank you, Peace. That is all that I needed right now. Thank you so much for being here for me—like a best friend.

Thank you, sweetheart. Sweet heart.

Dearest Peace,   June 25, 1995

Mia's graduation party is over. It is a huge relief. The thunderstorms that were predicted all week came this morning. They sounded beautiful, because they waited. Mia's day was lovely, she was lovely, everything went well. Today, we have likely sold our house.

When last we spoke, I was a little disturbed or uneasy about the feelings that had come up in regard to freedom. I don't feel a real desire to pursue it at the moment, but trust that you will lead me to pursue those things necessary for me in the Now, and I am happy to do that with the issue of freedom.

Earlier, I had the feeling that Mary's angel would be called Trinity. Then I thought, perhaps her angels *are* a Trinity. So we could look at that, if you like, but I feel no burning desire there, either. I wonder if I have other angels, but I love talking to you and feel no desire for more right now, so we can talk about that or not. Then I found kind of a new good word. I had bought this very weighty book called *Being and the Between,* which is full of jargon I don't know the meaning of. I was looking up *univocal,* which isn't in the dictionary by the way, and found the word *unity.* I loved its meaning:

> 1. the quality or state of being or being made one: oneness 2. a definite quantity or combination of quantities taken as one or for which one is made to stand in calculation 3. concord, accord, harmony 4. continuity without change (~of purpose) 5. reference of all the parts of a literary or artistic composition to a single main idea 6. totality of related parts *syn* solidarity, union, integrity.

Thought I'd look up *Trinity,* too, while I was at it. Capped it means:

> 1. the unity of Father, Son, and Holy Spirit as three persons in one Godhead. 2. *not cap:* triad, a union or group of three usually closely related persons or things.

Peace, I am feeling so contented today that we can talk about anything or nothing. Nothing is leading me to questions or concerns of the Now. Yet I would like to talk to you out of a place of contentment, to thank you for your help in the events that led to this day and this feeling. I am so thankful Mia had a good day and so thankful we have a buyer for the house. I am so relieved and yet almost emotionless. I am content to be. Thank you for my beingness, for bringing me to a place where I recognize it. Thank you for the good friends and family that made up my day yesterday. For my husband and children. For the breeze that blew yesterday, for the thunderstorm that waited, for all that is.

You create as you go, sweet heart. You had as much to do with the events and the feelings as I. More. But I appreciate your appreciation. I appreciate your wanting to be with me in a place of contentedness. Smile. Breathe. Appreciate the lightness of being. It is a good starting place for more. If you want more. When you feel content and unquestioning, you are open for more and more will come to you. You are not feeling like being active now. You can see it in the things you've said and brought me. This is fine. Don't worry that I will request of you something active today. Rest. But in your rest notice what it is to Be; notice the thoughts, dreams, imaginings that come to you. What comes to you in a state of contentedness is untarnished by desires, feelings, fears, active longing. Listen in your contentment to your inner voice, however it presents itself to you. Then, when you are feeling more like looking at and seeing these things, we will discuss them. Now. Go rest. Be. You deserve it.

Thank you, sweet Peace.

Peace, I'm back. I was drawn to a book, *Mavericks of the Mind: Conversations for the New Millennium,* interviews by David Jay Brown and Rebecca McClen Novick, that has been here forever, and I read all these great things that inspired me to come back. They're all from an interview with Carolyn Mary Kleefeld.[16]

And, Peace, this woman talks about everything we just talked about in a slightly different way! She says, "Ideally, all people would develop a self-referencing point to comprehend themselves and their universe well enough to guide their own vessel with awareness." Peace, *she uses our words* and *our meanings.* Everything from *in between,* to *vessel* to *possibility* to *circulation.* But most amazing are the words you just gave me yesterday! Just yesterday you said *vessel* was a good word for the stage I am at. You said I was a vessel moving through space, and she said a new book she is writing discusses the recordings of her "own particular vessel as it rides the waves of existence." You said I was creating space, and she said art creates the space to let what's possible happen. I can't remember you ever using the word *circulating* with me before, and she says, creative expression is a "unique circulation."

She not only used words from yesterday, but words from our first conversation when she said, "The ancient codes lie in the seams *between* worlds. They only await the radiance of our conscious light to be illumined, *recognized.*" (All emphasis mine.)

Peace, I can't believe this! And suddenly I'm here wanting more. And if I can't find it here, I'll go to bed and feel the breeze and listen to the night sound and find it there. I just discovered the word *unity,* and she said, "Notice that the word 'universe' means united verses. When in harmony, life is a symphony of united verses." Peace, I know it's waiting for me! Some alternate universe. Uni-Verse. That's what it is—the something more! And knowing that I might not be able to get here and record it here is all right because I know I will find it, and even if I can't bring it back with me to me, it's okay because it's something more. What is it that makes me want to sing?

Sing! Everything is okay here.

Sing with my fingers. Fly fingers, sing fingers. . . . Weave the universe, invite it in, let it hum.

I'm with you, don't panic. Go with it.

Feel the universe. Let it all come together.

Don't analyze it—smoke it, feel it, breathe it.

What is a trip? A drug trip, a trip trip? A journey in a vessel. A vessel. Riding the waves of existence. Riding. Going moving energy feel it, pump it, circulate, ancientness, authenticity, "I feel as if I'm in touch with what I call the 'ancestral resonance.' This would be a poetic translation for receiving information from everything that's ever happened. Within one's every breath lives every beginning."[17] Beginning, circulating, pumping, ringing, singing, going, moving, pouring, soaring, learning, leaping, authoring our own lives, lives, living, sleeping, dreaming, doing, being, ISness, oneness, divineness, trinity, unity, universe, verse, vessel, More. Peace, water, bridge, dying, changing, transporting, porting, journeying, going, boing, bong, good-bye, buoy, bounty, country, earth, living, oneness, planet, pond, trees, earth, sky, water, soil, soaring, bird, life light, likeness, lightness, beingness, transforming, being, seeing, sleeping, sealing, dolphins, walking, talking, communing, lowering, rising, rising, rising, rising, higher, higher, higher, higher, higher, clouds, spirit, angels, god, god, god, god, energy, all, that, is, is, is, telling me telling me telling me god is god is god is within with in in, in, in . . .

Dear Peace,   June 26, 1995
    What happened last night and what did I do up there?

Dear Margaret,
    What happened last night and what did you do up there?

I don't know. It was a random act of senselessness.

I don't think so. Why random?

The word just occurred to me. It just happened—randomly—there was no reason for it, no design.

Why senselessly?

It did not make sense.

But what did you think about it?

I thought it might be some kind of primitive communication; that was what went through my head. Kind of senseless, huh?

Why? Is communication with ancients impossible? You wanted more, you wanted to approach things in a new way. You wrote what went through your head. You were not trying to make sense and you were not trying to communicate. What goes through your head? Where did those words come from? Where do thoughts come from? The brain? The mind? What is the difference between the two? How can you prove that there is a difference? How can you prove that thought comes from the brain? Maybe some thoughts come from elsewhere. And, if so, from where? Where does love come from? From the heart? The heart has been proven to be a mechanical pump. Where is proof of emotion, where is proof of unconscious? Why did your mind, this time, give you a series of words instead of sentences and paragraphs? Or wasn't it your mind? Were you talking to me? to you? or to someone else? Or was someone else talking to you?

I tell you, all of it is true and there is no proof. In your dream you were in the Alps. Can you disprove you were in the Alps? Can you prove it? Your doctor told you today dreams don't have memory. Is he right or is he wrong?

I still don't understand it.

Margaret, it simply was. Words. Words were. Words came to you and you recorded them. You had a stream of consciousness. A stream. A flow. A river. A sea. A peace of the universe, a piece, a peace. Words flow. Where from? From you. From your desire to record. Re-cord. Re-establish. Links, linkages. With all that is. Is this mysterious? Yes. It is. There will be flows you will not be able to record but they will record you. They will become part of your signature. Yourself.

Peace, I feel a need to write my impressions of what has occurred thus far. Am I trying to analyze what should not be analyzed or am I trying to synthesize?

Trying implies analysis. Trying and synthesis do not go together well. I suggest you read, digest, and then let transformation begin the synthesis. You are wanting your knowledge to come together into a philosophy, a way of being. This is transformative. This is more. Just remember to make whole rather than to fracture.

Strum, hum, sing, dance when the universe calls you to do these things. Practice, participate, play. Your fingers tried to play the keys last night. Perhaps they were just not fast enough to catch the light.

Okay, Peace. So when I feel contentment, as I did last night, I am close to a place where *more* can happen. You were right—I knew I was. Then I found this remarkable writing by this woman I'd never heard of before. It was an incredible feeling, more so than with the other things I have read. It felt like a link. What then was I supposed to do?

Feel the linkages. We are all one in the universe. You and she are linked. Link-ages. A link with the ages. It is a living universe, Margaret.

Linkage: the manner or style of being united; the quality or state of being linked; a system with links (like Xs?).

PEACE

Linkages are the in between, Margaret. Trust the in between.

There is much lately about unity.

Yes. Oneness: unity. It is the goal. It is not just words, dear one. Unity is real, the linkages you feel are real. How else do you explain these words that are so close even though you never saw them before? If Carolyn had written, "I am a woman," that would be different. It would be a statement. But she was talking about discoveries along her journey. You, too, are on a journey. Perhaps they intercept, connect, link. Perhaps you share knowledge in more ways than you know. How does the mind operate? How does it come up with its words and images? Partly it is chemical, but partly it is alchemical.

I want you to imagine the possibility of there being real linkages between you and people you have never before met, such as authors of the material you have read. You do not always know why you do the things you do, but as I told you before, that is changing. Who did you write The Ninety-Seven Days *for? Perhaps for someone you are linked with though you do not know it. There are forces at work in the living universe that cause you to be the instrument and the musician. One day you are playing for all the world to hear, one day you are playing for one other to hear, one day you are being played. And always there are ripple effects. You may right now be writing this as part of a divine plan that will awaken the divine music in another. Nothing you do is without purpose. That you don't always know the purpose is part of being alive. Part of being. But I say again, you will not much longer act without knowing why you act. You are becoming conscious.*

Yes. I am becoming aware. More some days than others.

174

With awareness comes intentional acting; not cumbersome, not pro-grammed actions, but acting with knowing your intent, your purpose, for what it is you prepare.

What about avoidance? I find myself so often avoiding even things I know I should do or should want to do.

What you call avoidance may be procrastination, it may be not doing something you do not want to do, or it may be avoiding the dance, it may be holding back, it may be turning away from the recurring verse you need to hear to be free. Know the difference. Know yourself. Relax. You are doing fine. You cannot force more to come. But it will come.

Thank you, Peace. I love you.

CONNECTION

July 1, 1995

I cannot believe it is July. My busy season at work. The final month in this home—no longer truly mine. The last month I will write at this desk in this small corner of this universe of my old home. And yet the feeling I have today, that I have had virtually all day, is one of sweet contentment. I am aware of how "right" things have gone for me, and I am so truly grateful and so truly blessed. I feel, in a very real sense, that things have gone "right" because of the journey I am on, because of my being open to possibilities, because of my new inner calm. I feel just as certain things cannot always be so "right," but it's wonderful—full of wonder—this notion that my own "rightness" has caused the "rightness around me." I know I have not chosen the correct word here, Peace, but I thank you again and again, that I have found my way to this place, this day, this contentment in this moment of time or beyond time. This Nowness.

Our last conversation led me directly to *The Tibetan Book of Living and Dying,* by Sogyal Rinpoche. It led me to a course of expanding my connections, my living connections, to encompass those of great spiritual teachers. And it has led me to a study of meditation—of, as the author says, bringing the mind home. *Home.* Now there is a word of many meanings. None of which I will bother to look up in my contented state of mind.

I have done good work today: I have come home and taken a shower and put on my most comfortable clothes. I have bought a bottle of wine. And whatever happens tonight, I am content to be with. I suspect, however, that I will be back.

July 2, 1995

How can I describe the experience of last night with any

words other than pure contentment? My husband, my mate, my love, and I sat on the porch talking, touching. We were content together and if it was for one night, it was enough. We talked much of the new house and some of the old, and then he, sweet romantic, put on *our song,* "Always and Forever," and we made love while the fireworks sounded in the background from Taste of Minnesota. It could have been a movie scene but it was my own.

When we had parted from our lovemaking, Jimmy Buffett came on the stereo, this man my husband identifies with and plays so often that his music feels like background music to my life. It was vintage Jimmy we sat and listened to from the porch. And Donny came out with a gem of wisdom about complaining. He talked about how people didn't used to complain all the time and how it is only fashionable, today, to complain, and this is why people do it; and how he would hope to change that fashion in the people close to us. Perhaps it is our joint mission: to make it fashionable to be content and joyous!

Then, still on the porch, still sitting quietly, he said, "We should go to church tomorrow." He was so right, so wise, for we have been letting work on the house interfere with church. And Father talked about the miracle of Jesus filling the nets of the fishermen, and how He called us all to be His disciples to net men, to bring them the light, the news, the word. And Father talked of how we all have a

177

mission—we just have to find what it is! It was lovely.

And now, today, I get to spend time with my sister. And I get to put money down on my furniture, furniture that came to me as if it were meant to—the furniture that I had cut out of the paper and hung over my desk as my dream furniture. And it just occurs to me now that this is what was said in *Ask Your Angel*. To make a visualization of what you want. I did. And it came to me. At 50 percent off, at a price I could afford. And it cannot even be delivered until after July 31, the exact date of our moving. How can I be grateful enough? I almost fear how well things are going, but I will not allow myself to entertain this fear.

I tried to meditate on the porch before my husband joined me, and when I sat in alignment, it felt right, like a posture I was coming home to. And I realized instantly the meaning of carrying meditation into your *samsara,* your real life, as my husband joined me and we touched and talked and had mostly silence and love between each other.

I know good things are coming to me as I open my mind and heart to goodwill. And if bad things were coming to me, as I'm sure they will one day, perhaps I can remember this time and never let them shake my inner content. Thank You, Lord. Thank you, Peace!

July 4, 1995

The most important things coming to me are the teachings in the books I am led to read. I just read, for instance, in *The Tibetan Book of Living and Dying,* about *bardo*. *Bardo* is a Tibetan word that simply means a "transition" or a gap between the completion of one situation and the onset of another. *Bar* means "in between," and *do* means "suspended" or "thrown." In between! The natural bardo of this life encompasses the whole period between birth and death—making the period between birth and death a "transition." It says this life is one of constant suspense and ambiguity and that this constant uncertainty contains, by its very nature, gaps, spaces in which profound changes and opportunities for transformation are continuously flowering—if, that is, they can be seen and seized.[18]

I feel I have been led to this book in order to better understand the in between with which you originally introduced yourself to me, and perhaps me to myself. Is it possible that I am currently in one of the natural gaps, in a space between this life and the next, this life being the one of my first forty years and the next the one of the upcoming forty? That I am in a natural bardo state in which profound changes and opportunities for transformation are presenting themselves?

I am only your guide, Margaret. I cannot reveal your life story. You are creating it every day by everything you do. But can you doubt that you are in a state of transformation? Are there not things about you that will never be the same as they were last February? Or even yesterday? Who is to say that it was not the insight that you were in a phase

179

of passage that brought you to me and to the readings initially?

You may see that I am less willing to answer questions—if so, it is only that the questions you ask are growing more farsighted. In the state when your questions are farsighted, your most appropriate counselor is your own heart. You are approaching the phase of synthesis, in which you are to put together all you have learned. Look at the wisdom and insight of your recent writings. They are the goal. What comes from within is the goal.

As my guide, Peace, what then is your role?

To show you the in between so that you can see what can be found there, so that you can learn what is to be learned there, so that you can integrate your knowledge into a whole. You are not outgrowing me but you are becoming ready for more.

Is there another guide, Peace, who is working with me or who will work with me through this next stage of synthesis and transition to wholeness?

There are many, many guides, dear one.

I only ask, Peace, because of this feeling that something new is coming, something different, something to help me with the next stages of my study with meditation and with becoming more fully conscious and because I can't imagine what this something new *Is*. You keep telling me the time is coming when I will no longer act without knowing why I act—perhaps the biggest compliment you could pay me—and I know it will only come with my ability to remain conscious in the present, with my ability to stop and think before I act.

Not to stop and think. To always have an inner knowing that guides you—part of which is me. And it will come from always being conscious of what guides you—part of which is me, but the much larger part is your open heart. It is the integrating of wisdom into a self which is able to accomplish this constant open beingness that you are wondering about. It is the infinite possibilities of this next stage that excite you even in your calm core.

There are two things going on here. One, this something more you seek is within yourself. Two, you are uniquely suited to this means of communication. It comes naturally to you. Meditate to quiet your mind. Come here to express it. Don't get the two mixed up.

You see the light of the computer reflecting back to you—and I tell you, you reflect back to it. Do not mess with this, do not mix it up. You see the smoke hit the reflection and dissipate. This is what your spirit guides are like. A consciousness joined with your own, not separate, not the same. You are the vessel that contains the consciousness. Like a clear glass of water, it can be seen through, but that does not make the water any less real or the glass any less a container or the liquid any less fluid or thirst quenching. If you think of yourself as this clear glass vessel and your spirit guides as being contained within, unseeable, or see-through-able, does this help?

It reminds me a little of the Buddhist description of karma as the consciousness that remains between one life and the next. It is not the individual, not each memory, but the piece of ourselves we only catch glimpses of—the true consciousness (which I am hoping to develop) that continues. The essence. In this sense, then, of your being part of my consciousness, you could be part of the former self?

This is true in a way. Would it be within your ability to understand that you might have a spirit guide who was once yourself? Would it be beyond your understanding to realize that all beings are part of self? The concept of reincarnation accepts that the consciousness, the mind wisdom of a great teacher, may become the mind wisdom of another great teacher, a teacher who has all the wisdom from this life and, within his or her consciousness, all the wisdom of past lives as well.

Is this why I am struggling with concepts of rebirth? Because I am afraid of the consciousness I have brought forward from past lives, afraid of that pain or humiliation or failure?

If there were those things, could you not learn from them? Can you not cease to fear them? Let fear go. The more you seek cannot get through the barrier of fear or self-denial. Accept all of self—past selves and future selves, then you will be ready to know your other spirit guides. Go and rest and contemplate—what can you not accept? When your answer is nothing, when you are open to all that is—to truth—then we will go forward in search of more. It is a great discovery—a great journey—if you let go of your fear.

SERENITY

D earest Peace,   July 6, 1995
     Mary used a good word for what I felt most of
the day today: *serenity.* Then as the day wore on, the
serenity was pierced by tension. I came home and felt
serenity again, and then an argument with Angela
pierced it again. I have not yet, in the throes of tension,
learned how to pull myself back to the place of serenity.
Can you help me see the way to do this?

The way to do this is to come to all situations from your place of seren-
ity and, when you notice your serenity leaving, call it back. The point is
to notice it when you have it and to notice it when it is leaving. Are

there times when you should not be serene? No. This does not mean that from a place of serenity you cannot argue, but you can argue without losing what you have if you notice that what you have is leaving. Like a friend whose helping hand rests on your shoulder, notice serenity, and notice when the hand is removed. Ask it to return. It will return. You simply have not yet remembered, in times of stress, because you need to practice.

You are becoming better at controlling the stressful situations you encounter when you are alone, but you are not practicing when you are with people. You let the energy of the other person pull you from your place of serenity, like someone shoving away that helpful hand that rests, RESTS, on your shoulder. That hand is not guiding you or pushing you. It is at rest with you. Calm and placid, something like the brick propping open the door to your heart. Inactive yet accomplishing its mission. You have many times visualized your open heart. Now visualize your helping hand as well.

Thank you, Peace. I know this will help. But what can help me with the aftereffects of tension that settle in my stomach and so are carried into the future even when I would like to return to serenity?

I would like to tell you to meditate, but I know you are having trouble finding a sacred place in which to do this. So first, I will tell you to make a sacred place in which to do this. Make space for it. You cannot go on forever hiding your spiritual journey. There is a fear that keeps it under wraps and a habit of keeping yourself under wraps. A habit that brings you some self-satisfaction, like your smoking. You use smoking to take a break. You can use meditation also. Quit kidding yourself that

184

smoking and break-taking are private things no one knows about—you know they are not. Start thinking, at least, of letting your family in on your secret. It is not something to be ashamed of, and sharing it will not make it less personal. More is more. The more you share, the more you will get back. This is an important lesson about "more" that you need to know and that you need to act upon.

Thank you, Peace. I needed to be reminded of those things, also. It is hard to imagine how I will be in the new home, and I know that how I will be is my own choice and my own making. If I state that I want to meditate every morning in peace, my family will respect my wishes. If I choose a "place" to smoke, my family will accept it. I am still afraid to ask—to make my wishes known.

You were once afraid to make your wishes regarding furnishing your new home known, also. Sometimes wishes come true to show you that wishes come true—if you let them be known. It is like the joke about the man who prays to win the lottery and when he confronts God after many times of not winning, God says, "You could at least have bought a ticket." Contrary to what you believe—or you wouldn't act the way you do—your mind cannot be read, your desires cannot become a burden on others, whether they are known or whether they are not known. Ask and you shall receive. Remember this. And ask. Not just here, not just God, but there—with your family and friends, in your life. Let others bring you joy. More is more. What is brought to you, you will return.

GUARDIAN ANGELS

July 9, 1995

I have been feeling as if the more I search for a "way" and a "method" to reach enlightenment, the farther I am getting from it. Then I read in *Healing Words,* by Larry Dossey, a little story about the writer Natalie Goldberg. Apparently, she had a Buddhist master, Katagiri Roshi, here in Minneapolis with whom she had studied for years. Then she moved away, did a lot of writing, and came back to see him. She asked him for more lessons and he said, "Don't be so greedy." He said, "Writing is taking you very deep. Continue to write." She said, "But Roshi, it is so lonely." And he asked, "Is there anything wrong with loneliness?"[19] He admitted that he was lonely too, and that the point was not to let loneliness get in the way, that anything we do deeply causes loneliness. It just is what is and must be accepted.

I had been reading *The Tibetan Book of Living and Dying* and put it away in favor of *Healing Words*—possibly because the strongest message of the *Tibetan* book is that you can't approach spirituality with a shop-around mentality. You have to find what works with and for you and stick with it.

I did not take this to mean that I should not read, explore, investigate, but I came away with the feeling that I have what I need: writing and Catholicism. I think back to how Thomas Moore and Joseph Campbell and James Hillman started me on my quest by touching something in me that resonated, something that felt profound and right. And how glad I was that these teachers were of my faith. Even many of my favorite quotes from other books were from monks, saints, and Christian contemplatives. Even if it does feel lonely sometimes, I think the moral of the Natalie Goldberg story, as it applies to me, is that my spiritual quest is what it is and I need to accept it. That I know what is right for me: my religion and my writing.

Perhaps they are one and the same.

Yes. Thank you, Peace. Perhaps they are. I guess I *know* that there is no place where I am closer to the divine than here—right here—with you, but not just because of you. Because here is where my higher consciousness speaks. I am not ruling out meditation or any other form in pursuit of enlightenment, I am only opening myself up to the possibility that my meditation takes place here, in the pauses, perhaps.

Oh, yes. You are finding what is right for YOU! You are taking the leap into personal realization.

And I am seeing that I can have desires and have them met. I have furniture, drapes, towels: I am building the house of my dreams, as part of a team with my husband, who is honoring my desires because I have made them known to him, because I decided what I wanted, because I let my desires be known to me. I am beginning to make decisions, to know myself well enough to make decisions. Where furniture might have seemed a simple thing before, it suddenly is not. Or to rephrase that, furniture is simple, but building a home that honors my desires, honors my family, is a holy task—which makes the furniture, the drapes, the towels, a blessing. I am thankful for each piece, from washcloth to couch. And I realize that this is the way it should be. This is how we should live. The spiritual journey is becoming the life journey, part of every facet, every decision, every waking hour and in the hours of dreams.

I was just looking something up in my *Lives of the Saints* book and found the term *Guardian Angel* and the fact that October is the month of Angels and the Rosary. I did not know this before. The feast day of Guardian Angels is October 2. My book says:

The angels are pure spirits endowed with a natural intelligence, will, power and beauty, far surpassing the nature, faculties and powers of man. The angels number millions and thousands of millions around the throne of God; praising Him and serving Him as messengers and ministers, and as guardians of men on earth. . . .

Those blessed spirits who are appointed by God to be protectors and defenders of men are called Guardian Angels. Faith teaches us that each individual has a Guardian Angel who watches over him during the whole course of his life. It is also a generally accepted doctrine that communities, the Church, dioceses, and nations also have their tutelary angels. The Guardian Angels . . . endeavor to keep us in the right path: if we fall they help us to rise again, encourage us to become more and more virtuous, suggest good thoughts and holy desires, offer our prayers and good actions to God; and, above all, assist us at the hour of death.

Prayer: O God, who in Your unspeakable Providence have deigned to send

> Your holy angels to watch over us, grant
> Your suppliant people to be always
> defended by their protection, and to
> rejoice in their companionship forever
> more. Amen.[20]

Ah, Peace. There it is. My own religion telling me exactly what I have found in you. And what a lovely prayer, to ask to *rejoice* in your *companionship* forevermore. Ma would be happy that I have made use of her little book. The Word, being passed down generation to generation. This is such wonderful permission—and it was here all along. As you were here all along! As my religion, my faith, was here all along! That you endeavor to keep me on the right path. *Yes.* That when I fall you help me rise up. *Yes.* That you encourage me to become more virtuous. *Yes!* That you suggest good thoughts, *yes* and *yes* again. That you suggest holy desire. What were we just talking about? *Yes!* Peace, you are my guardian angel?

Yes, dear, I am your guardian angel.

I am even learning, Peace, not to balk at words like *suppliant*—inactive words that I used to think implied lack of will and weakness. I now know they mean the opposite. I now understand what surrendering to a higher will means. It means to be!

You have been a good pupil, Margaret.

You have opened my mind and my heart. I am eternally

grateful, and I am beginning to think that eternally means eternally.

It does, dear one.

There is so much more I need to learn. Somehow I am certain you will lead to where I can find.

All paths lead to home. All wisdom comes from within. Together we will find your wisdom, layer by layer. Think of wisdom as the petals of a rose. You have been collecting them. Why? Outside of time and space you knew they would connect to your journey. Your layers of wisdom, like shades that block the sun, are being peeled away. Now you might think—peeled away *implies "getting rid of." It is good imagery because much of wisdom is indeed getting rid of*—*getting rid of those things that block your ability to see and be.*

And Angela started the rose petal collecting.

You know she is a visible link for you to view the connectedness of the universe. The two of you can be in tune enough to speak without language. This is not a great accomplishment, however. The great accomplishment is in seeing that as you and Angela are connected, all are connected. As deep as your compassion flows for your children, the world is like your children and your compassion will be as deep as the river. Your prayers are your thoughts and your thoughts come now from a place of knowing within. Your thoughts, thus, when compassionate breed compassion, when angry breed anger. It is very important for you to remember not to act, think, speak without knowing. The days when you did so were like your adolescence. These days are not days so much when you are grown up, when you are big, but when you are open. And just as you are open to receive, you are open to give. Try sending a message of calmness and peace to your spirit sisters. Write it below and see what comes of it.

To Julie—as we prepare for our students' arrival, do let go of worry, do let go of fear, do let go of rushing, do trust that you can depend on people, that people love you and will not judge you. Be. Be in a state of calm restfulness. Feel your breath come more freely. Feel the tense muscles that hang on let go. Let love embrace you. Believe in love, including the love of your father. Let it soothe you.

To Mary—as you gave me the word *serenity,* let serenity now rest on your shoulder. Give yourself permission to suspend judgment, to be in a place of serene restfulness with the events of last summer. Let Grace rest within your heart as she rested in your womb. Be her gentle mother. Take care of yourself as if you still, in taking care of yourself, are taking care of her.

May you both bring your restful calmness, your quiet breathing, your belief in self, with you into our busy season. May you think of it as a time of connection with your spirit sisters and so with your spirit. May you view these coming days with an attitude of "what will be will be and all will be as it should be." Let us all turn from the illusion of control and let go and Be. Amen.

LIVING IN A WORLD OF PLENTY

July 11, 1995

We're two days into our on-campus session and there have been two miracles. The first, and I say "first" because it happened to me, was this: I asked Donny to get me one hundred dollars to use as change for student fees because I had forgotten to stop at the bank. I needed the one hundred dollars to be in fives. He said, "The cash machine doesn't give fives." And I know he saw himself running around to different stores exchanging the money he got from the cash machine for five-dollar bills. But the cash machine gave him twenty five-dollar bills. The second miracle was that Mary's step-daughter, Amanda, saw Grace. She saw a toddler sitting in a chair in the backyard and saw her vanish into white light.

I came tonight to have a conversation like we used to have, when you did more of the talking than me! I've been hogging the white space lately! I came without questions in mind. Now I wonder if the miracles are the question. I believe my miracle was the same as the miracle of the furniture and the drapes and the house and all the good things that have been happening to me in my new state of openness. Mary's miracle is different, and perhaps it is hers to hold to her heart and not for me to examine. I just wondered if there was anything you wanted to share about them.

Mary's miracle, like your miracle, is one of the open heart. These are the only kinds of miracles. The Grace miracle was a miracle of love. Grace allowed this miracle to happen through the open door of their love for each other. It happened through Amanda to bond Amanda and Mary with love. Love creates miracles as love creates the universe. It is just that the universe is such a large concept. Does believing that everything is one make it a smaller concept? Are small miracles not miracles?

I get so nervously excited when you tell me things like this that all thought seems to leave my mind.

Your mind is the conduit. Its flow will not always be even. You are not an electric company, after all. You are a dear, open heart.

This makes me think of my dear husband and how when

I have been too tired to give him physical love, I have tried to telepathically send him spiritual love, a love I send from the open door of my heart, outward like a wave of light. Does this have effect? Does he feel my love?

Why not ask him instead of me? All love goes out like waves of light. Your visualization only intensifies it, directs it. Try directing it into the universe sometime. Try directing it to the trees and sky. Try opening up even wider—to the all that is. Experiment, practice, and above all have fun. Take joy in giving love—in sending love. You've been thinking a lot about your Aunt Alva. Sending her your love. I won't tell you she knows this, but I tell you that you cross her mind as she crosses yours. Think about it. Crossed minds.

My very first book, a book about Grandmother Ivie, was going to be called *By Heart*—for the process we have of committing things to memory, to remembering. It just struck me, the profundity of those words in the new scheme of my wider understanding. *By Heart* and *crossed minds.* They are very similar. Word symbols that almost give me goose bumps.

Your words. In the beginning there was the Word. You are on the right track, the right path, with your words. You are using them as they were meant to be used: as symbols to express the divine. Words are nothing more than miracles of the mind.

They don't compete with silence do they?

Silence without words can be complete understanding or the totality of loss. Silence is silence. Words are words. There is no competing.

When there is competing, as there was at work today, what is the best way to deal with it?

It takes two to compete. If you do not compete, it will not touch you. Your stumbling block away from serenity is people. It is true for many others. Monks withdraw for this reason. Serenity is easier in alone time. Easier is not always better. Practice carrying serenity on your shoulder. Soon it will just be—not easier, not better—it will just be. The goal is to Be.

Healing Words, by Larry Dossey, talked about how surrender is very active—because it has to be done again and again—and about how different it is from giving up. Do you have anything to tell me about surrender? Is that what I'm doing? Is it like having the courage to change the things you can and the wisdom to know the difference?

Your inner view is what creates change. In a constantly changing world, what is change but the status quo, the norm? Efforts to make change are thus a contradiction. You live in change. The only moment is Now. How you view the Now is how the Now will be. HOW YOU VIEW THE NOW IS HOW THE NOW WILL BE. You have felt this. To have experienced this is to know reality. If you surrender to the Now with love in your open heart, you are very close to home indeed.

Peace, is my next step still to find joy?

Are you not finding it? Do you not recognize it? It is not something profound you seek. Do not go on looking. Look within. Open the door to your feelings, smile! rejoice! This moment is joy! Let it fill you.

I am kind of a circumspect individual, Peace. You are right that I have joy in my life. I don't have to be exuberant about it, do I?

You can't clutch it to yourself, either, sweet heart. If you clutch it to yourself and bury it back within, you will smother it. Let it out! There will always be more. You can let it out quietly, sweetly, with your sweet smile, with your kindness. But you can't clutch it to your chest and say, "I have joy now and it's mine, all mine." That is not the nature of joy any more than it is the nature of love. Feel your joy and let it radiate out from you the way you are letting love radiate out from you to your husband. Don't be a miser. Remember to leave all those collecting-of-resources ideas behind you. It is not the furniture that will make the home. It is the love. You cannot collect joy and love and miracles and hold them to yourself. You can only let them be in the moment. The miracles are there to bring you joy to bring the world. Share, sweet heart, share.

A part of me is still fearful of all the good things that have been coming my way. If I were to get a publisher now, all my dreams would be coming true. It is almost as if so much good has happened, I don't dare wish for more, and I fear something bad will happen to balance the scales.

Forget scales! Forget balance! Forget limits! The universe wants you to be happy! Go ahead, be happy! Don't let fear tap you on the shoulder with its whispers of "bad follows good." HOW YOU VIEW THE MOMENT IS HOW THE MOMENT WILL BE. There will be difficulties. There will be struggles. It is not as if you haven't had them now. You are very busy. You have money worries. You have all the

197

difficulties of a normal, busy life, and more. And yet you have miracles and joy! You do not need perfection. There is no perfection in the duality. There is no need to fear.

I cannot repeat strongly enough—the universe, the all that is, wants you to be happy, wants you to realize you live in a universe of plenty. You are doing your part now to make it so. And so it is. Forget change. In your world, nothing lasts forever. Enjoy the Now. When fear taps your shoulder, tell it your shoulder is already occupied with serenity and tell it to move on. There will be challenges that test your serenity, big ones and little ones. But you will be ready for them. Your happiness is safe. It is your time to become safe in the world. Trust this. Trust each moment to be what it will be.

July 17, 1995

I have been away too long. Today I only want to say hello, to say thank you, to say how glad I am you are with me throughout the day, to say thank you for the gift of consciousness which helps me remember that I am a being of love. Thank you, too, for your last message. It is often not until I review my messages that I see how dear they are to me.

Mary, who is now communicating with her angel frequently, has talked with me about this need to review messages. One or the other of us is always coming in and saying, "I got a great message last night," but unless we have it printed out, we can't remember quite what it was, or at least can't *convey* what it was. We both have to go back to the written words to repeat them to ourselves without the interaction. It's as if we really "get it" when we're in the midst of it, but then, until it is reviewed, all we can say is that we "got it." We can't explain what it was we "got." It's as if when we're receiving the messages, we're caught in the power of it all and it all makes sense and it's all wonderful. And yet afterwards, we are left kind of drained—sometimes a joyous drained, sometimes a melancholy drained, sometimes a hopeful drained, but almost always *drained!*

Often, I feel as if I expect too much. Sometimes when I ask something of you, I do not feel, initially, as if you have given me a very clear answer. But when I review your answer later, I recognize that you have given me the only answer, the answer that is perfect for me. Not, perhaps, the answer I wanted. But the *answer.*

Often I await profound wisdom, complex wisdom, instead of being satisfied with the simple. And yet the simple is so profound. Like your telling me that it is my time to be safe in the world or to trust each moment. These are profound simple gifts and truths that I can't be grateful enough for. Thank you for all my messages, for me and for others. Help me to combat things like jealousy, envy, tiredness, competitiveness in my work and my relationships. Thank you in advance. I love you.

Hello, Margaret, and good night. Remember to rest and to smile and to be open. You have much to learn from this wider experience of people and cultures. Don't limit yourself. Don't forget to be open. Don't be afraid to ask. Seek and you will find. Honor your work and it will honor you.

TRANSITIONS

I have been very busy but busyness has not diminished my desire to concentrate on this spirituality. The spirit sisters are beginning to plan a day together away from work, and the mere thought of a day to spend together sounds like a feast, a banquet. It seems an amazing thing that has happened to us. Three ordinary women. Three middle-class, married, working, struggling women, about as different, other than as women, as we can be. It may be that we have the ideal environment for what is going on. It may be that wishing for a more ideal environment is folly. Yet I've had recurring dreams of a retreat house.

Perhaps it is your own home—your new home—that will be a retreat for you and for others.

Is there anything you can tell me about the coming direction of things?

I can tell you not to push for a direction. Go with the flow. Rest. Rejuvenate. More is coming. The move is the beginning.

Is there some way I should ritualize the move? Make it a thing of ceremony and beauty?

You will. It is one of your strengths. You will not forget the importance of this time. Look for beauty. When you have a choice, choose beauty. And do not be hurried into acting without thinking. Let ideas flow. But rest and rejuvenate before acting.

July 21, 1995

As our moving day approaches, I live more in the future than in the present. Even disregarding the move, it is the future my thoughts are drawn to. What will be important to me in the coming months? Writing? Learning? Traveling? Homemaking? I had an idea of writing for a grant, using this piece of work I have created with you as a means to request time for a sabbatical for me and Mary and Julie, perhaps with a guide, to show the world what three ordinary women can do and become.

I may not speak overly much of the spirit sisters here

but you know that it is because what happens here also happens there—at the office—when I am with them. It is as if here "it" happens on this computer with *you*, and there "it" happens in conversation, in sharing what has happened here, in *being* together with *them*. As if they are the divine manifested in my daily life.

I think of so many things, all bounded by time, bounded by the job, the move, the trip. I will go with the flow, but I also know these ideas are occurring for a reason. I know ideas are one of the things I need to let flow. I am surprised at how often my ideas are about *us*, as in the spirit sisters, rather than just about *me*. I am more certain than ever that what is happening with *me* is bound up in what is happening with *us*.

My biggest fear, whether about me or us, is that I will not act when the time is right for acting. Time again. I was getting away from time, Peace, and now I am being drawn back in. Some of which I know is the result of the busyness of work. Can you tell me how I will know when the time is right, when I need to act? It is hard to get my ideas around being and letting go and going with the flow and still seizing opportunity. Will opportunity be going with the flow? As I move away from things of the mind to things of action, the concepts we have discussed become less real to me, more ephemeral. Or perhaps it is only being away from you.

Or perhaps it is only being away from you. Remember to ask, Where am I here? Where am I in this moment? In this flow? Yes, you have to live your life, do your busy work, but you do not have to do it on auto-matic pilot. Being aware in the moment will bring richness to the moment, will make the opportunities present themselves, will let you see them. Will let you seize them or them seize you. If you do not act with-out thinking, you will not act wrong. But revise your idea of thinking. Thinking is not planning. Thinking is not simply ideas. Thinking is understanding. Thinking is knowing self. Think of thinking as being aware of the moment. Being aware of what you are doing. Being aware of what you are preparing for.

What you are feeling is the end of much preparation and the begin-ning of a time of doing. Thinking about how to do what you will do will not necessarily help you. Think more about why. Make choices. Do not act on automatic. Act from the heart and the gut. Move, flow, from one thing to the next with love. And as you do, there will be choices that present themselves to you. You do not know that you will be working the same job next year, so why worry about it? You can know only today, and even today is not meant to be worried over. Remember while you do things why you do them, do them voluntarily or choose not to do them. Feel yourself flow with the moment.

Thank you, Peace. More later.

Yes, dear. MORE later.

July 23, 1995

Dear Peace,

I have not had a profound experience of you in quite some time. I have not used candles or incense to invoke a mood, and I have not had time alone in which to approach you. I am now alone for a few minutes, and I would like to return, in feeling, to the closeness and mysteriousness of our earlier encounters. That this form of communication comes easily to me does not, in my heart, make it right that it should come to feel commonplace and devoid of mystery. I ask you once again, with the sincerity of a beginner, of a seeker, to come to me and be with me and speak with me. Not out of any great desire for answers, but out of a great desire for a feeling of the divine to once again come over me.

I have reviewed thoughts in my journals from my past, from a me I can still identify with but who is not the me of today, a me who felt empty and alone, a me who struggled to survive and who searched for reasons to survive and for some cessation of the emptiness. You have filled me, Peace. I went to church today. I heard about the path and about the few who find light in the darkness. Your light has filled my emptiness, yet I return at moments to a loneliness perhaps inherent to being a human being. It is from this reminder of emptiness, from this reminder of longing, from this reminder of loneliness that I call upon you. Will you join me once again, dear Peace, and as my Guardian Angel bring me good thoughts and help me rejoice in your companionship?

Stay steadfast, Margaret, in your turning toward the light. There may be a time to visit the place of emptiness you once knew, but this is not the time. To remember loneliness, to experience loneliness is a primal place, a place of beginnings. You seek a return to the mystery of beginnings. Every day is a beginning. But you need not return to primal aloneness. You have experienced the light of oneness. I am with you. You will never be alone again.

Thank you, Peace. Thank you for bringing me out of the primal beginnings.

To the path. Together you and I have identified the path. A simple path. A path of love and Nowness.

And of communication?

And of a communication deeper than communication. To communion. To union. Out of the duality of beginnings into the in between of union and connectedness. You wanted, today, a reminder of connectedness. You wanted a respite from your human path of busyness. Here it is! You do not always have to rejoice in an active way in our companion- ship. Quiet communion is companionship of a higher level.

Thank you, sweet Peace. I have wanted to lay my head down in weariness.

To be comforted. To be quiet. To pause in the in between. I know, dear one. Pause. Relax. Ask and it shall be granted. Seek and you will find.

Will you help me find some quiet in the busyness of the Now? Can you assist me in ridding myself of this cough that must sap some of my strength? Will you show me the will of the higher power?

Good girl. Ask and ask. Ask as much as you like. There is no formula I haven't given you. There are no instructions you do not already have. But when you ask, you become open to receive. Do not be afraid to ask.

I am about to move and I will need to contact my agent, Dan O. I have been afraid to ask him for an update, fearing, of course, that he will say go find another agent. I guess I want to ask you to assure me that this will not be his response. But I won't do that. I do ask you to guide me in my communication with him and to guide him in his communication with me. Can you do that?

I hear all your requests and my hopes are your hopes within the path you are bound to travel. Why not tell Dan there is More? He cannot read your mind. Your writing is your truth. Do not be afraid to ask regarding it. Do not be afraid.

Which "more" do I tell him about, Peace?

Simply tell him there is More and let his response guide you. Put your feelers out. Be receptive. See what comes. You will not have to struggle for what is coming next. It will happen. It will flow. If you let it. If you let the universe provide for you, it will return the love you are trying to give. Approach all you do now with your open heart and with your awareness so that you do not act without understanding why you act, what your purpose is, what you prepare for. Then the best that can come to you to fulfill your destiny will come. Pray. Ask. Love. Release.

July 28, 1995

I was thinking about how little I have read lately that resonated within me, and thus, how little I have had to bring to you in regard to thought-provoking questions. I feel in some ways you have dodged my questions regarding my "writing life," despite your reassurances that what goes on here is good and is truth. I have taken this to mean that you refuse to predict my future. But if you can offer me guidance at this time, I would appreciate it. As I just wrote in a letter to Dan, the move is a time of new beginnings and although I do not foresee myself moving in and sitting down to write within the week or maybe even the month, I am hopeful for a direction to present itself to me.

Write what you are compelled to write. Follow your bliss. This is where you will feel the rewards of your writing. Do not think of writing and outcome together. When you think of outcome, your writing will not come from the heart. I have and will continue to advise you—do all you do from the place of your open heart and you will be rewarded. Inspiration will come. Inspiration—to breathe into, to breathe life into. New home, new life, new breath, new inspiration. Leave worry behind like the old home. If you leave worry behind, inspiration will come and with it its own rewards.

Dear Peace,   July 29, 1995

The girls are at the Maronite convention in St. Louis, my busy season is over, Donny is not home from work, we close on the new home in two days. It is time to pack. Perhaps even this computer. It is time to leave behind this corner, this dark, damp, basement room that has given me so much light. I am overwhelmed by the tasks ahead of me and that is why I think of packing my computer earlier than is precisely necessary. I think of this because the time for contemplation here, at this site, is drawing quickly to a close. I am entering a time of action, of packing and cleaning and physically relocating. And while this computer is here, I am drawn to it and to you.

Just this afternoon I had a Grace experience and was able to share it with Mary. I was standing on the loading dock smoking and thinking about a student's presentation on the ethics of keeping children born with serious health problems alive to have a quality of life most of us would think is not worth living. The student had brought doctors in to visit one such home for these children to make them ask themselves if sending a patient home alive was always the most important thing. And I was thinking of telling Mary about this when a brilliant yellow butterfly swooped down before me. I believed it was Grace or a message from Grace.

In this busy time, I have been far from experiences of Grace. But I am at an open place at this moment, in which truly anything can happen. I am without a plan of how to pack and how to move and what to do first, second, and third. Part of me wants badly to devise such a plan, just as I have come here to announce that this will be the last time we talk in this place even when it may not be. I am in a state of suspended animation, even with you, struggling to envision how things will continue. In a week, where will I go to be with you in communication?

And yet while I say I am open, I know that a part of me is not. I do not come here with the open mind and heart of the woman who has been writing to you for so long. I do not know what has happened; perhaps there are expectations where there were none before, fear where there was no fear. For in this state of transition, where and when everything is changing as you have assured me it does moment by moment, all of the time, I am anxious and uncertain. I welcome any message you have for me. I welcome especially the feeling of you. Please come to me in the in between of this time, this time that I am grateful for and yet fearful of.

Hope. Go back to your readings on hope. To your writings. Hope is possibility. Limitless possibility. Your new home will be what you make it, not with a plan and a list but with an open heart. And not only your new home. Your new you. Remember, you are a child of God. Your possibilities are as endless as life itself. Let your spirits rise like smoke, like hope. Feel the lightness of being that comes over you. Smile. Laugh. Be happy. This is truth. When people say "true happiness," this is of what they speak. You have little experience with true happiness. You will have none if you do not lighten up. True happiness is a reward you cannot turn your back on and cover with anxiety. All those times Felicia said, jokingly, "I can tell you're really happy" when you were showing no signs of it, are an example. Let yourself be happy. Let yourself be. Let yourself go. Let go. Shed yourself of fear. Shed yourself of worry. You know things will get done. Allow yourself this.

Your landscape will change. Like life after life, you will still be you. What do you want to be? The essence of you. The real you. The you who has an open heart. Go to the center, the circle, the boundlessness of who you are. To the peace. Go forward from a place of peace. Leave anxiety behind. I will help you and I will be with you. Think Peace is with me *whenever your anxiety awakens. Is this not the Now you have hoped for? Your busy season is over, the move begins.*

It never occurred to me before, Peace, but when you just reminded me to tell myself, "Peace is with me," I thought of my dad and how, when I was growing up, he was always saying, "Peace be with you." It sounds so prophetic now it makes me want to cry. My dad, my earthly dad, telling me all my life, "Peace be with you." And here you are. With me. Part of me. As I'm sure you have been all my life though I did not know it. It makes me feel better as I get ready to begin. I just have to get started. Once the journey is embarked upon, it will move forward on its own.

You have embarked on the most important journey of your life, the journey to the center of the self. All other journeys are a matter of putting one foot in front of the other. Believing you are safe. That you will be on solid ground. Only the spiritual journey requires you to leap. To leave the solid ground behind.

But my journeys are combined. Intertwined. A web. How do I leap across the precipice on the one hand, and take small steps on the other?

One is human life, one is divine, the web is the in between. Think of the in between as being where Peace resides. A foot in both worlds, with Peace in between.

And Peace is both you and a feeling.

And Peace is both me and a feeling, and they both are one and they both are within you. A place, a concept, an emotion, an alternate reality. Truth is in the in between. The in between is within.

Treat me as a child for just a moment and let me ask, What should I do next?

Begin. We all begin anew once more. We all begin anew. Begin. Dig in. Get into it. Immerse yourself in it. Begin anew. With each step you take, feel yourself beginning anew. Go for it!

You have more energy than I have at the moment, Peace.

You are wrong. Your energy is limitless. Beginnings are limitless. They are energy at her most intense. The big bang. Energy released. Poof! Heaviness gone. Lightness emerging. Begin, begin.

> Begin: to do the first part of an action, commence, to come into being, arise, also found, originate, invent.

YES! Come into being!

July 30, 1995

Thanks for yesterday, Peace, I felt better after talking to you and had a better day today. My mind is full of concerns like carpet and cupboard liner and paint. Coming here helps me remember why my mind is full of these things and what it is I prepare for. Not just a new house but a new beginning in a home that will honor me. It has, in the waiting, almost become a presence, and I do feel as if it is waiting to welcome me. Please be with me, tomorrow, Peace, as I open the door and cross the threshold for the first time. Be with me in my activities—activities that may not include this computer for a while. Be with me in my cleaning and painting and gardening. Be with me as I turn preparation into action and still my mind for moments of peaceful reflection. Help me to create, especially in my sunroom, a sacred space full of mystery and light, calmness and energy. Guide me to those things of beauty that will endure, that will be part of the simpler, less consumptive life in years to come because they satisfy and lend contentment to my life. You have taught me to ask, and I am asking, dearest Peace.

Hello, Margaret. Welcome back. Today you are once again open and receptive in your asking. You are asking without fear because you are asking from a place of knowing. When you get to that place with your writing, you will be ready to ask and receive. Your path with your new home is clear. It is about combining the earthly and the divine. It is about accepting the duality of this life in a place of serenity in the in between. Take your time. Give yourself as much space as you can. Look at your home not as spaces to fill but as space in which to be. Let yourself Be in it as much as possible. Let it fill you with its presence—a living energy that is unique to it. Combine your uniqueness with its unique energy. Meld, web, integrate, transform. It, too, has a spirit. Place has spirit. Yard, grass, trees have spirit. They will welcome you. Recognize them.

Dear Peace,   August 6, 1995

I have been almost a week in my new home. I have scraped wallpaper, scrubbed floors and woodwork, shampooed carpet, painted. David cut the grass and I pulled a few weeds. Angela has been my constant companion. Mia

212

and her boyfriend, Chuck, come in the evenings. Donny's parents, Katie and Ed, spent one day with us. New carpet and wallpaper are ordered; the furniture will arrive at midweek. I spend my breaks with a cigarette on the back steps. The freeway already bothers me less. I want Father to come and bless the house.

I think most about you and my spirituality when I am taking a break in my yard. Yet the empty "spaces" of the house work on me. The neglected smell of six months of emptiness is leaving, the smell of paint and Lysol replacing it. We have pushed back our move-in schedule by one week. It is for the best.

Tomorrow I am to return to work. The busy season seems aeons away. Work itself seems unimportant. I have noticed the single-mindedness with which I go about my work at the house. I set a goal and it is all that's on my mind. It is almost therapeutic, as is the physical work. Sometimes, especially when I am cleaning up after others in the new house, I get a feeling for my new role, and it is one of "grand" mother, in the way of powerful mothers of the past—the one about whom the family centers and gathers itself, the one who holds together the life of the family.

My spirit sisters have been absent from my dreams but my dream life has been rich, including everything from wallpaper to Jimmy Smits to Jack Nicholson. Each time I come here feels as if it may be the last, Peace, the last in this place. And as my reading has become uninspired and close to nonexistent, so has my questing for answers. I come to talk to you almost not expecting an answer— our connection seems weak, as does my connection to the spiritual. And yet, I know my life is forever changed by the events of the first half of 1995, and I do not want the journey to stop.

Please return to me, dearest Peace, and grant me your assurances that when I leave this place for good, I will still have access to you.

I am with you. Dearest Margaret. You cannot escape me. There will be times when you will try to turn aside your spirituality. You cannot. It is within. Think of the word channel.

> Channel: the bed of a stream; the deeper part of a waterway; strait; a means of passage or transmission; a range of frequencies of sufficient width for a single radio or television transmission; a usually tubular enclosed passage: conduit; a long gutter, groove, or furrow.

You worried, when you asked for Mary and Julie, about the power of being a channel and about the responsibility. Think instead of the beauty, the symmetry, the flow of it. Honor it. Be grateful for it. Pray. It is a flow. From you to me, from me to you but both at the same time, like a river flows, always there and always moving, a place, an idea, a movement. Like thoughts that can't be grasped or proven, but surely are. The communication is always open, dearest. You can block the flow but you cannot stop it. Moving with it is the safest, surest way to navigate it. You are always there. It is always part of your actions, from the simplest to the most complex. Transforming the mission as you move to fulfill your destiny.

Thank you, Peace. I love you, and I am forever grateful to you and to this communication.

You are welcome, Margaret. Go in Peace.

Dearest Peace, August 8, 1995

We are *really* packing today, Peace . . . me, Mia, Angela, Chuck. And it's happy. We're getting along, listening to Creedence Clearwater Revival; the mood is just right. Thank you to all who are watching over me and have been watching over us in this move. Donny and I had our first almost-fight yesterday. It has blown over. The new house is taking shape. The transition is almost complete. I'm overjoyed to feel this close to you and to be feeling this good about the move. I think I needed to feel close to you again before I could move with *peace* of mind. To feel close to you is to know you come with me. Despite what you told me, I had to feel it in my innermost being. Now I do. Thanks. Do you have any advice for me, dear friend?

Don't pack all your memorabilia away. Put it on display. Don't worry about where it is to go now—just think of its storage as temporary. It is time to surround yourself with the memorabilia of your life. Let it be open. Share it. Most of all, don't worry.

I like the idea of putting my things out. In fact, it gets me kind of excited. Thanks for the idea.

215

PEACE

Let go of your worry and the things that will please you will become apparent. Also the things that will please your husband and children. Don't try to control things. Let them flow and everyone will feel better. Rest when you're tired. Work when you have energy. Laugh with your children when the mood is carefree. Enjoy! It is time to enjoy! Remember that joy is your lesson in this time. Good things are coming to you. Accept them with joy. It will all come together in a way that pleases you and your family if you do these things. That's a promise. Yes. Smile. That's what pleases me the most.

Back again . . .

I can't believe how much *stuff* we have. Consumption has to stop. There is only so much stuff one house can hold. Even one like our new house. I know I'm supposed to leave worries behind, but the thought of having all that storage space and not having enough storage is ridiculous. I must have forty suit jackets and I don't even care to wear suits anymore. And yet, can I part with them? I don't know. It seems so foolish. Both having them and parting with them.

If I had something to eat, I think I'd just sit down and eat and then go to bed. Tomorrow will come and we'll move and I can't worry about it. I'm writing here now just to have an excuse to sit down. I know you don't mind. On to folding clothes, packing CDs, finishing the kitchen. Then pick Ang up at work and get something to eat, and bed. Thanks for everything today, Peace. And thanks for the dreams!

You're welcome, Margaret. Rest well.

Dearest Peace,   August 16, 1995

Well, today is the absolute last day I will talk with you from here. The last of everything comes *home* with me *today*. Last night, Donny and I shared what felt like our first night in our new home. We finally got the drapes up, and afterwards, about midnight, sat outside together. It reminded me, as it does each time I sit out there, of traveling. The nights have been humid, the air is full of the sound of crickets chirping, and in the background is the noise of the highway—just like at the many motels at which I have stayed in my travels, both as a youth on the way to and from my grandmother's house in Georgia, and as an adult, as in last year's vacation to South Dakota. Those memories are all wonderful to me and so are the memories being made in these first days at our new home.

We sat together in the cool humid air, Donny shirtless, and I leaned against his cool skin and we talked quietly and had moments of intimacy and relaxed for the first time.

As I walked in the nearby park this morning, I thought of you telling me to look for beauty, and it's there in the paths and on the lake but no more so than in my own backyard. Thank you for all of it.

The kids are going to be here any minute. Is there anything you want to say to me—any last words—from here—before I disconnect?

PEACE

Go in peace, Margaret. Go about your life and your spiritual quest in peace. These are words that have been with you all your life. Remember them. Yes, a spiritual quest can stir waters that have been long still. But the object of the stirring is to come to a peaceful rather than complacent stillness. A peace in the Now, in whatever you do, with whomever you're with. A peace of spirit, a peace that comes from the center of the being, from the center that has been forever and will be forever. A peace to carry forward into the next life. A peace to carry outward to others. But a peace, mainly, that fills the being. The limitless being. Go in peace, Margaret. Carry the Peace of me within as I carry you. We are all interconnected in peace. Go in Peace.

I V.
BEGINNING

IMAGINING

August 27, 1995

I am writing from my new office—my new home. It is in a corner of a damp basement (if you can believe it, I let my husband appropriate the sunroom for the TV) and I don't care. It feels so good to be back. I sat down, pulled up the Peace file, and there it was. It felt almost miraculous to see it here, in this new house. In this new house where everything has come together so beautifully.

I have learned to find a simple grace and quietude in the smallest things: winding extension cords, cleaning or cutting endive, things I do with my hands. But this is the biggest, the grandest, the happiest. Peace is here! I have read the whole Peace file, and I am moved by it, by my own innocence more than my knowledge. I haven't thought of myself as innocent since I was thirteen. There is a sweetness about the Peace file—from the first day when I was told to smell the sweetness. It is the sweetness of innocence, of teacher and pupil. To read it is like learning to read all over again . . . the knowledge, the excitement, the adventure. The love of words! I cannot begin to say how much it all means to me.

And so, here I am, about to ask Peace to join me once again, putting it off only so that I can wait until I have a quiet hour with no pressure to do other things. Because I know Peace is my still, quiet voice within and I know he has led me and will continue to lead me to breakthrough moments of higher consciousness and greater creativity.

I have begun to say affirmations from a book I just bought, *Higher Creativity: Liberating the Unconscious for Breakthrough Insights,* by Willis Harman and Howard Rheingold. Those affirmations are:

> I am not separate.
> I can trust.
> I can know.
> I am responsible.
> I am single-minded.
> I have no other desire than to know and follow the will of the deepest part of myself.[21]

And I realize that this is letting go. Turning events over to the higher self, the unconscious, surrendering, if you will, to the will of God.

And this is where I am at. This is my beginning in my new home. Happily, contentedly, surrendering, letting go. What a relief!

I cannot wait any longer. Welcome Peace! Welcome back! Welcome home! It's me, calling you home. Will you answer?

I am here and I am happy to be with you. I am smiling. We are not Home, but we are home on earth, home in the physical, home in well-being. Safe, comfortable, surrounded by beauty. Home. Peace on Earth.

Thank you, Peace on Earth, for bringing Peace to my little piece of it. For bringing yourself here. This, too, is a relief. You're here! My eyes fill with tears of joy to have you here, to have what we have here continue. Thank you. Welcome.

You have learned much in our break.

I have tried (for want of a better word). I have been mainly involved in the physical, but as I said before, as it comes together it has risen to a higher level.

Yes! It has living spirit. Like the words that come together to form a beautiful philosophy, a living message. Everything is coming together.

Is it, Peace? Is everything?

Everything has come together for you to the point of trust. Why trust?

Because you have decided to let go. No. Not decided. You have let go. With your innermost being you Know, you Trust, that you can let go. I could not force it upon you with my words. You were the only one who could make the choice. And you did it now, today, on this time of our rejoining. Hurrah for you, dear one. You are one step, one giant step, one leap, closer to Home.

I didn't even realize I was going to surrender until I did, until I had, and the relief flooded me. I think it was an unconscious decision as much as it was a conscious one. I think this is the way it is supposed to be.

That is the goal. To let go and let your highest self, your connection to all that is, do the planning, the deciding, the choosing for you. It is not not you. It is the best you. It is us. It is from oneness. You and the all that is connected. Linked. Xed. Joined.

This is so new to me. Now what do I ask you, dearest Peace?

If surrendering has lulled your curiosity, it is only so that you can rest in the relief. Rest as you have never rested before. Rest, and in your resting will come the stirring of the still, quiet voice, the voice that asks for more out of a whisper of calmness rather than the raging of necessity, desperation, frustration.

I have no other desire than to know and follow the will of the deepest part of myself. . . .

Look deeply and there I am, reflecting back what you are.

What is the will of the deepest part of myself, Peace?

Curiosity already? Before rest? All right, dear Margaret, I will give you something to think about in your calm restfulness: What is relief? Where does it come from? What emotion is it? Is it from your head or your heart or your soul? Or is it a relief that spans the entirety of your being? And if so, what more is there to your being than head and heart and soul? That is the plane we will be on now that you have surrendered, now that you have let go. Sometimes I will have to remind you that you have let go and we will need to spend some time unraveling the ties that have bound you up once again, but when I am not reminding you, we will be communicating differently. On a higher plane. As if from a mountaintop with the sun shining on us and a clear lake reflecting the image down in the valley. Visualize a new reality from which your relief springs. Leaps! Rejoices! Be light in being, as in the opposite of being heavy, and be light, as in luminous. Let your light shine. Let your relief be like a beacon. A safe haven in a stormy sea. You will see that others will be attracted to your light. You will learn from them and develop a new curiosity about service to others and to the universe. You will sing, you will write; released of burdens, you will float. The higher Will will reveal to you the next steps, the next leaps.

Are you my higher will?

I am, you are, and so much more. You Know this, Margaret. I am your comfortable companion, your guardian angel. There are so many more to guide you, dear one. Now that you have surrendered, you have announced to the universe that you are Ready! Ready to be taught and aided, ready to teach and aid. Ready to be a light to all, both heavenly and earthly beings. You are now connected on your journey to all who have surrendered on their journey. Arms linked, you could circle the globe. Light linked, you could circle the universe.

Can we bring this down to a more earthly level for a minute, Peace?

You make me smile and laugh out loud. Hear the heavenly music. Is it your daughter and the stereo or is it a choir of angels? I tell you it is both. At this very moment a choir of angels is rejoicing in your surrender.

But you wanted me to come down to earth. I smile and smile. You have made me so happy tonight. Just imagine, dear one, a life without struggle. I know you are thinking to yourself, No, that cannot be, but I ask you to imagine it. I ask you to imagine waking up and doing what you want to do every day. I ask you to imagine your children as happy and healthy as you could hope for them to be. I ask you to imagine your marriage continuing as happily as it has been but on a deeper level. I ask you to imagine your relationships with all your friends being on a deeper level. I ask you to imagine your dreams of being a published writer coming true. I ask you to imagine a car that will be like a transport to the clouds. I ask you to imagine an international trip filled with love at every turn. I ask you to imagine intimacy beyond any you have ever known. Is that earthly enough for you, my dear?

It is more like heaven.

Exactly. Imagine a heavenly life on earth. Nothing less. And go on to imagining this heavenly life on earth coming true for all those dear to you. And imagine the number of those dear to you growing infinitely greater. To bless is to increase. You will go through life blessed, *increasing the capacity for life in all of those around you. Again, you wonder, a dream too good to be true? Do you not trust the universe, the collective power of beings such as myself? I have told you many times the universe wants you to be happy. Imagine it and it will be so.*

Okay, I'll imagine it. But I am still only human. I still have the day-to-day, hour-to-hour "stuff" of life to deal with. I don't mean to rain on your parade, I want everything you mentioned, I love that you want it for me, I even believe it has a chance of happening, but I still don't see myself having that deep inner stillness as a constancy. I can come here and hear all these wonderful things and feel wonderful and feel relief, and then I go upstairs and act the same way I always have.

You have only just made the choice, dear one. Give yourself breathing room. Give yourself space. Give yourself relief and restfulness as a gift before you think of the minutiae of life. Do you think you cannot have all the happiness and success I described and still be human? And still be crabby occasionally? Yes, you will increasingly find a calm center. But it will come from your relief. Don't block the relief, the huge relief, with small worries.

Okay, Peace, I will *be* with my *relief.* I will imagine with my relief. I will leave the minutiae of life behind for a while. I will float through water instead of walking through water. I will be grateful for the relief. I thank you and all that is for it. Just help me achieve my calm center, okay?

Let relief calm your center, okay?

The dictionary defines *relief* as removal, lightening, release from duty, elevation. Okay, Peace. Why do I feel like one step forward, one step back?

Because you are not accustomed to relief, to joy, to imagining having what you want. It seems too easy to you. It seems beyond belief. You are trying to will yourself to believe instead of staying steady in your relief. But it is a momentary setback. Let it go and go back to relief. Stay there as long as you want. Rest there. It does not mean you can't come back here, that we can't continue to explore marvelous things, inner things, outer things. You are worried, aren't you, that I have taken away the quest that has become something fundamental to you, something you enjoy? Dear one, this could not be further from the truth. While you are resting in your relief, your unconscious mind, your higher self to whom you have surrendered, will be doing your work for you.

This is a foreign concept to you, I know, which is why you have struggled to let go. But you have let go, as you have opened your heart. I am the keeper of the brick and, if you will, the keeper of your surrender. I didn't think I would have to remind you of your letting go so soon, but I will remind you as often as you need. You have turned your burdens over—not shirked your duties. There is no law that says you must struggle. It is only the conditioning of your upbringing, the illusion your unconscious mind will help wake you from. This is the lesson of joy we spoke of at our first meeting. Let the relief grow in you and it will turn to joy. Be at peace with your relief, sweet heart.

Remember the sweetness of the journey you read about here only today. Imagine all you can imagine without struggle. But first rest in the relief. I cannot say this strongly enough. Give yourself space to rest in relief. Do this, dear one. Then we will talk again. Believe me, you will get used to it. You will say, "Why would I struggle to hang on to all that struggle when Peace was telling me all along I could let go?" Now, go rest in relief in your new home.

August 29, 1995

I am crabby, crabby. It is PMS. It is wanting to control things in the new house, to have others take care of it the way I want them to. It is not having my own space that has a door, that has privacy. It is wandering around the house wanting to smoke and having nowhere to go now that it is so buggy out at night. I have gotten lovely rest and lovely dreams. I go to work and stay mostly uncrabby. I come home and I am crabby again. The systems aren't functioning smoothly yet. The girls don't clean as I'd like, Donny doesn't pick up after himself, the garbage people didn't come, we haven't figured out the recycling, the cats shed hair everywhere and get on my furniture. I just want to stay home and take care of my house. I want to hear from my agent. I want to rest in relief. Yet I continue to struggle. And, of course, it's hard not to feel guilty about being crabby when I have this wonderful new home and this wonderful spirituality and wonderful sleep and dreams. Peace, HELP! What's the matter with me?

Your body needs to catch up with the rest of you. You, the real you, are inspired—you have received the breath of hope and spirit and freedom and divinity. Your body is still living with the old you. Your body is demanding some attention and you're not listening. You don't want to listen. You are afraid of what its demands may be—from quitting smoking to getting exercise to meditation. You are happy to work on your mind and soul but the thought of body work bores you. You're in a time of manifestation. Wanting the inner you to become the outer you. You're being directed in this just as you have felt inner urges that directed you to begin this file, to pray, to read. Listen to the still, small voice. Otherwise it starts to scream.

That's how I feel, as if I could scream—about everything, everything that doesn't go the way I think it should.

You may hate the thought of body work but you love the investigative process, the discovery of new knowledge. I'd like to propose something. Why don't you tell me a few words about how your body feels and tell me why you think it feels the way it does, and then we'll start trying to find ways you will like to have your body catch up with the rest of you. You don't have to worry that I'll ask you to give up smoking. I won't ask you to do anything you are not ready to do, and I can perhaps give you suggestions.

All right. It's as if everything inside me is under pressure and, although you have told me I've released, I feel as if there is no release valve. Just pressure. That's the main thing.

First of all, wear purple tomorrow and as often as you need to in the coming days. Purple is the color of manifestation. It will remind your body of your new spiritual state.

Remember to breathe. Breathing deeply will help release the pressure and will remind you of your inspire-a-tion. Go and buy those foods

*you want to eat now. Get your new contacts. Your clear vision is impor-
tant now. Spend as much time as you can among the trees; you need
their energy, and if you breathe deeply when you are with them, they
will use yours as well. Look for the Aramaic book of meditations. Listen
to soothing music. Repeat your affirmations. Imagine having the body
you want. That is enough for now. To imagine it is enough. By imagining it and giving it to your higher consciousness, some ideas that you
will like may come to you. And some miracles may take place!*

Thank you, Peace. I feel better already. I do. Whether it's
because I had alone time with you and smoked five ciga-
rettes or because of what you told me or a combination, I
don't know, but I feel better.

Today is the anniversary of Grace Zuri Love's death,
Peace. I dreamt of a baby last night. I wonder if this
anniversary of her passing has anything to do with either
the tension I feel or the dream.

*You are feeling some of Mary's tension. Because you are connected,
you have taken on some of her energy as your own. Tomorrow will be a
better day. Believe this. The cycle is complete now. Mary's relief is
coming. You can always call upon Grace to help you through difficult
times, as you can call upon anyone, living or spirit, if you call with an
open heart and are open to receive their aid.*

It is hard not to think of Grace as a baby.

*At our core, we are all the same: ageless and eternal. Grace's personal-
ity was strong and sweet and loving; that it did not have time to reveal
itself doesn't matter. As a baby, she was strong and sweet and loving as*

she is now. Spirit is what goes deeper than personality. Smoking may be part of your personality now, but it is not part of your spirit. You will not smoke in your spirit form. And you will not miss it, I promise you.

Okay, I read you. Thank you so much. I forget to be grateful sometimes with my personality. My spirit is always grateful. Good night.

I smile upon you in your sleep. Rest in relief, and imagine!

Dearest Peace, August 30, 1995

It is the end of another very long day but one in which we at least had dinner. We even sat around the table after dinner and discussed music and Jimmy Buffett and dreams and what inspires. Thank you, Lord! We needed to eat dinner and have table talk. It has calmed something in me that all the spirituality could not calm—it calmed my humanness.

I probably would not be here tonight if it weren't for Julie. Today she asked me to ask you what the heck is wrong with her. She very humorously tells of her steps backward—the tension and gritting of the teeth, the strain she is under. And she asks: How do I get out from under it?

So I took her request and stored it away in my brain and, in the late afternoon, at cigarette break, I started getting messages, I think. They went something like this: When does Julie have time to be Julie? That the answers have to come from Julie but they can't while Julie can't connect with Julie. I heard that she needs time free of responsibility on a regular basis. That she is a systematic and organized person and needs a systematic and organized way to go about her quest. Things to that effect, anyway, after which I know my own mind got in the way and embellished your basic guidelines with thoughts like, *Yeah, she should get some time to herself, a baby-sitter, more help from her husband.*

So I'm here to see if you have anything clearer, more direct, more inspirational to say to her than my, "Yeah, you should get some time to yourself." I know that the "When does Julie have time to be Julie?" came from you. Is there anything else?

Tell Julie to have a dialogue with herself. What is at the center of Julie? Who is she? In the busy life of a young mother, it is a lot to ask. It is almost impossible to detach self from mother. But ask her to try. Ask her to make space for herself in which to be just Julie and then to have a conversation with herself. What can Julie say about Julie's nature, wants, desires, dreams that are about Julie alone, separate from everyone else—not just children and husband but mother and father and work and friends.

This may sound confusing because I am always going on about our connectedness. But the connectedness works best when each person is fulfilling her unique individual destiny. It is like a net where each filament is intricately bound to the next, and in the end it is one piece and serves a different purpose, with each part holding its weight and none stronger or weaker than the other. None stronger or weaker than the other. In trying to be the strongest link, Julie may actually make other links weaker or become weaker herself!

233

Tell her to think of the universe, the all that is, the angels that protect and guide her as her safety net through which she cannot fall, cannot escape, cannot become lost, cannot be hurt, and upon which she can rest as on a swinging hammock under the open sky. The universe is here to cradle her. She need only lay down her burdens and rest.

However or wherever Julie can find her restfulness is the beginning point from which she must befriend herself and find out all there is to know about herself, as she would want to know all about a new friend. Think of it almost like a courtship. Each discovery will only cause her to fall more in love with self. When she is in love with self, she will have made half the journey and will know the path to complete it. Tell her I am aware that this is not new advice, not the timeless wisdom she seeks. But the timeless wisdom she seeks will be found on the journey inward.

Thank you, Peace. As always, you say the simple things with beauty and profundity.

September 3, 1995

In four months, we've written two hundred pages, Peace. Makes me a more prolific writer than I have been on my own. But I'm about to get back to it—to *Who Killed the Mother?* It's Labor Day weekend. Angela goes back to school Tuesday, Mia and Donny go to work, and I have a day off! I'm hoping *Who Killed the Mother?* will just sing to me on Tuesday, Peace. I'm feeling very ready to get back to it, very hopeful about it, and yet pretty peaceful as well. Whenever I get anxious about it, or more specifically,

The Ninety-Seven Days, I try to remind myself I've turned it over to my higher power. My subconscious agent, my agent in the sky.

I slept for fourteen hours yesterday! I must have needed it. I know you keep reminding me to rest! Today I'm going to take care of a few practical matters, like getting myself a chair. And at the first opportunity—a family dinner, the *next* family dinner—I'm going to talk about the help I need from the family both to keep the house clean and to get my office ready—that is, to get a room with a door. I keep thinking it was part of the bargain on buying this house, and I will remind myself that bargaining has nothing to do with love, and this is to be a labor of love like everything else having to do with this house, this home. There is still much to do in everyday matters, as there is in my spiritual life.

I have been without something compelling to read the last few days, which is probably good, as it gets me back in the mood for writing. But I do hope to buy a book today. I have thought a lot about imagining. When you were telling me the wonders that awaited me upon surrendering, you kept saying "imagine . . ." At first I took you too literally, as if you were saying these things will come about, not "imagine" these things will come about. You were giving me something active to do, not saying these things would be done unto me. And I've found how important imagination is in a different context. I remember reading something by Sam Keen in which he talked about how he goes along day to day and then something like seeing a father cradling his dying son in Bosnia on TV will make him stop and imagine how it would feel. And because I was thinking of *imagine* in a new way, I suddenly saw how imagination is the start of everything. If we cannot imagine how another feels we cannot have compassion. If we had no image in our minds of Africa, our knowledge of Africa would have no impact on us. If we could not imagine there would be no discovery, no invention, because humankind would accept what *is* totally.

And so, while I've come to a new understanding of *imagine,* I've also come upon some messages of duality. First, I have surrendered and given over my desires to a higher power. Then you tell me to imagine. I'm not sure I know how to imagine without will, without worry, without turning imagining back into desire. Second, we are told to be in the Now and to accept that everything *is,* yet if we stayed completely in the Now and accepted everything in its ISness, we would not imagine and discover and invent—would we?

Everything Is. This does not mean that human beings are aware of all that Is. Accepting all that Is does not mean denying that there are things we cannot see. It is accepting and embracing the mystery. Imagining Is. Like Knowing. Like Trusting. It does not come automatically in its true form because of the illusion and habit of culture and upbringing. I told you before, in your childhood you had a rich life of imagination. Being forced to grow up too soon altered your ability to imagine. In writing, you

236

have forced your way back to a life of imagination. But it is still not the imagining of your youth. The imagining of your youth was innocent and pure. Imagining for the sake of imagining. Imagining for fun! You invented stories and whole worlds for the sheer joy of it!

You are still a novice at joy. You are still unsure of your footing in the world of joy. Perhaps it is because of your old view of imagining. Imagining is not about will or about willful desire. It is about joy, first. It is about going back to the lessons of childhood when you saw with fresh eyes and you saw equally as much with your imagination as with your sight. When I told you your sight was going to be important, I was not kidding. Because you are being asked to go beyond "regular" sight. You are being asked to imagine with fresh eyes, with youthful, innocent eyes. How can you See possibilities with eyes so grounded in reality? Go back to hope—hope being the loving and limitless possibilities a parent feels for a child.

See the possibilities. Imagine them! This is very important. You wonder how imagining is different than Seeing the possibilities. And yet when you heard the word Hope *used in this way, as a way of seeing limitless possibility, you thought you understood how to Be! You said yes! You were excited. If you cannot get your thoughts around the word* imagine, *it is only because of the pain of childhood and the forgetting that childhood pain caused you to do. If you cannot imagine, See the possibilities. Imagine the possibilities. Sight and imagination.*

You talked about being able to imagine Africa. Can you see Africa with your eyes, with your sight, without the benefit of television or photographs? No. But you can see it in your imagination. Open up your idea of sight to include imagination. It will enrich all of your senses and your compassion as well.

You want me to be less literal.

I want you to Be. To rest in relief. Leave literal behind for a while. Leave reality where it's at: at the body level. Let your spirit soar! That is all I am asking, all that I am trying to get you to achieve. And yet you hang on so tightly. You cling to your reality. You look to science for verification. Fine. Do so. But come along with me too. Don't be forever letting it pull you backward. Make a leap of faith. If you do not believe, how can you surrender? What do you surrender to? I know you believe. You know you believe. In the God of your youth, in the All that Is. Is it only my teachings you chafe against? Or is there something you are afraid of? Meditation? Then don't meditate. But do open your eyes, imagine, see, believe. Have convictions. Believe. Believe what you believe. That is all that is required. Just as I say "be who you are." That is all that is required. It is all one, isn't it? I can tell you a million things but when I say "be who you are" it is all the same, all one.

Perhaps that is the problem. Perhaps I am not in tune with myself at the moment. Perhaps I am just in a state of flux. I have lost the tension or most of it since I got my period. And I am restless because I haven't a good book, something new to sweep me away to the next idea. I am so darn greedy, Peace. I am always after more. And what I like best are books that condense it all for me—take all these teachings and put them together and then say, see what it all points to? That is what I like. Not to be told this is the way, or I've disproved this way, but the openness of all the teachers I've encountered. I'm uncomfortable with those who say this is or this isn't. I'm comfortable with possibilities. You were right about me there. Does this mean I lack *conviction,* the state of being convinced; belief?

Sweet heart, relax. You are doing fine. You are content in the mystery. That is enough. You can believe in the mystery. I only ask that you remain open to it. That is exactly what I ask and you have led me to a good way to describe it. You believe in the mystery and, therefore, you believe in staying open to the possibilities of the mysterious.

Like the other day at work, when the radio came on by itself? All three of us spirit sisters were standing there when it happened. When it came on, it was nothing but static. Mary went to the knob and fiddled with it and we got a religious song about surrender—about putting oneself in His hands. And Mary and I looked at each other, sure that it was a message. (We had to tell Julie it was a message.) We were open to the possibility of the mysterious, and I told Mary, "Well, Peace told me he was going to remind me I had surrendered." Is that what you're talking about?

That's exactly what I'm talking about. Yes! Yes! That is all you have to hang on to—your openness to the mysterious, to the possibilities. That is all the spiritual quest requires. That is your conviction, your belief. I think it is a good belief. How about you?

Yes. It works for me. I understand it. It fits where I am at this time. It fits my Now. Thank you.

NEED

Today is my wedding anniversary. The day began with a dream. In it, I was floating on a raft in the sky, waiting my turn to fill the bird feeders there with birdseed. The teenage boy who was filling them ahead of me was walking on air. He was sweating and obviously finding his task both trying and exhilarating. It was a sacred duty and he was fulfilling it. He was to make two trips and then it was to be my turn. While I wanted to do it, I was afraid of doing it. I saw his effort and I thought, *I am heavier than he.* When it came my turn, I could not step off the raft. He made one more trip. Then when he came back and I was going to step off the raft and complete at least the second part of my task, we were only three feet off the ground. I had missed my opportunity.

It was a dream of deep feeling and poignancy for me. It also followed a day behind Mary Love asking me, "Have you asked Peace about your writing?" She asked this in the context of me talking about the Dan O. situation. I responded, "It seems as if I ask him all the time and his answer is always elusive, something like, 'It will happen when it is time.'"

And finally, Mary returned the books she had borrowed. One was the James Hillman book and in it I read: "Curiosity about fact and detail gives way before the open contemplation of what is, just as it comes."[22] And I feel slightly "wrong" about my curiosity, or better put, I feel as if I have been going about it the wrong way: with curiosity rather than contemplation. Curiosity, I now see, is about the details, while contemplation is about the whole. And so, while I am seething with questions: What did the dream mean? Does it relate to my writing? Am I missing out on some opportunity by not taking action? When do I know that taking action is right? How do I know? And how do I meld it all with the truth of having surrendered? I already know—just in this minute—that surrender is not about curiosity but about contemplation. And this new way of seeing gives me *hope* once again, because it helps me see how to *be* once again and particularly how to be within my surrender.

So I come to you with what I hope is a state of contemplation—a state not active but open—to hear what you care to share with me about this time and the questions, rephrased in the language of contemplation to be questions not of detail, but of how to be. I sit, my heart open to contemplation, prepared once again to listen. I await your voice.

The only movement is circular. The gold ring falls into the porcelain bowl and spirals. Its sound is clear and singular. It is an image borrowed from your reading. Reading that stays within you waiting for the moment at which it can be of use. It exists within you until it can be of use and when it is used, it is transformed. It becomes something other than what it started out to be. This is analogous to the godliness within you. It is there, waiting to be used and thus transformed. This is your writing, also, waiting within to be used and transmuted. The circle of life, death, rebirth is constantly occurring within you. Constantly. It is. No beginning. No end. No thought ever dies. It exists once it is thought. It is. But constantly changing: living, dying, rebirthing as needed.

My need to accomplish something with my writing seems to be greater than any other need I have. It comes up again and again, circular, unstoppable. Is it only ego, Peace? This *need?*

If you could meet your own needs, you would not be human, and yet you are the only one who can meet your needs. This is the divine. The divine may come in the form of another person, in the form of an angel, in the form of new thoughts, in inspiration. The one who meets your needs is the divine One no matter what form it takes.

242

Peace, I ask here, as I may not have asked before, for help in fulfilling my need.

Can you define this need for me, dear one?

Please, Peace, Lord, Ancestors, help me to meet this need. Is it a purely human need, Peace, as I was about to say it is? Is there no divineness in my cry to be heard? I want to say it is not about ego, and fear that it is. I want my writing to be wanted. That is what I want. I want that comfort, that security, that validity. Is there something inherently wrong in that? Is that why my need goes unfulfilled? Please tell me truthfully, Peace. Is it that the writing in and of itself is supposed to give bliss and comfort and security and validity even while going unwanted? Am I missing something important here?

My dear, you have stated your need. It needed to be stated. You want your writing to be wanted, you need your writing to be wanted. You have expressed your need for the first time, for the first time. Why do you now want to find something wrong with it?

Need has never been comfortable for me, Peace. I have not liked to need. I have particularly not liked to give expression to what I need. I resist it at every turn. Why, Peace?

Fear, sweet one. Fear is not a simple thing. It is not a pat answer. It is. As circular and unending as everything else. Need is tied up, for you, with survival. It is ancient. One needs air to breathe to survive. One needs food to eat to survive. Expressing a need is as ancient and eternal

243

as the will to survive. To live is to need. To be present in human form is to need. Can you deny yourself food and air?

Had to break to take Angela to her guitar lesson. Then my sister, Susan, came over. Then Donny came home with some friends. I realize I can't control things. I'm frustrated and I have to let it go because I can't control life, I have to accept what comes, but . . . where do you draw the line between acceptance, letting go, accepting noncontrol, and being Milquetoast? More on this later. The following occurred in my car while I waited for Angela. It was written in a notebook and transcribed here.

What do I *need* to know about needing? Once again I feel as if I'm missing something.

There are those who equate divineness as a cessation of human need. There literally is no such thing. To be human is to need—air to breathe being an example. Divineness comes in part, then, from trusting that there will be air to breathe. It would be difficult to function at all if this need being met were in doubt, as it is imperative that those who do not have food to eat make meeting this need their main function. This is one reason the meeting of basic needs is seen by all sane governments and people of power as an inalienable right. Because it is recognized that one must be free of this basic striving if one is to be more than this striving.

Your thought then, I need my writing to be wanted, *is an expression of your will to survive. And it is. It is set in its circular motion. It lives. But it lives the life of one who must seek each day the food necessary for survival because it does not trust that this need will be met. Needs are needs. They are not right or wrong. There are only needs and the degree to which we trust they will be met.*

The Catholic joke you brought up earlier about the man who didn't buy the lottery ticket now comes back to me. How do I know when to act and what actions to take? I am trying to tell myself this isn't the detail seeking of curiosity, as it probably is, but looking at it in as big a way as I can, in as whole a way as I can, I know I must write, I know I must trust, but then mustn't I also do? I had such a strong feeling that my agent Dan O. was going to be *the one* to bring my writing to the world. How do I know when to let go of that and seek elsewhere?

If your need is for people to want your writing, they first have to know it exists, don't they? Let it go, as literally as you have let go of other constraints and fears. Send it out into the world. Let it be known that you have a need to be filled and see what the universe sends you. Buy the lottery ticket and have faith. Trust that your needs will be met. Believe that they will. If your need remains a secret, your writing will remain a secret as well. People who can help you are in your life for a reason. Let them help you. Don't be stingy. Tell the world as you know it. There is someone in it who will be the right one. I will show you the way if you have faith and let go. The answers are waiting to come to you.

Am I to do anything with this writing, Peace?

You need your writing to be wanted. All your writing? Don't you think

245

there are those waiting for this writing just as you wait for those who want to read your writing? It is a circle, dear one, a living circle. Like your supply and demand, though I do not like to use words of commerce. Build it and they will come. Write it and it will be read. Sweet heart, it is as simple as that.

What about all those writers who never are published?

Trust that what needs to be will be. Think of the authors who have touched you. Their words were there to fill your need, your need was there to fill theirs. A circle. A golden ring falling into a porcelain bowl. A natural law of gravity causing it to spiral and sing. It is a golden ring until it hits the bowl. Then what is it?

Dearest Peace, thank you for your wisdom. Please hit me over the head with the map I must follow, the instructions on how to proceed. Peace, Lord of all that Is, ancestors, show me the way.

Dear Peace,   September 13, 1995

I spent a lot of time today thinking about needs. First I thought I had to voice my needs and that a failure to do so was a failure. Then I thought again. It is all in the approach we take, isn't it? Contemplation rather than curiosity, for instance. It seems to me that with almost all my needs, approach, the right approach, rather than the actual voicing, is what matters. Take, for instance, those small things around the house that drive a person crazy: if approached, as you have taught me, with the thought of "what is it for which I prepare?" the feeling changes.

And so I am looking for a way to respond to needs that doesn't come from voicing them. This may be a cowardly way of avoiding my "need to voice" but I do want to think it through nonetheless.

Even if some needs must be voiced, how must they be voiced? I know that I have voiced my needs concerning my writing, when I have voiced them at all, with fear. Fear of failure, fear of not being worthy, fear of ridicule, you name it. And I can't help but wonder if the same fear doesn't pervade everything. It is basically a fear of asking and being denied.

I remember when my sister, Susan, would come home from college and ask Dad for money and he would make her jump through all these hoops for five dollars. She was probably nineteen or twenty, and I was fourteen or fifteen, but I remember telling her that I had already learned it wasn't worth it. By that young age, I already thought that almost anything was better than asking. Independence seemed the most prized thing in the world. But I'm getting away from myself. Or maybe I'm not. Expectations, too, which you and I have talked about here, were, by my early twenties, something I had learned not to have. It seems as if, in sum, I grew up believing in a world of scarcity where my needs would not be met or the price was too high.

So, if I take it as a learned behavior, can I do anything substantial about it? What my original thought was, thinking more of relationships than writing, was that if I acted always out of love, if I remembered love in every situation, I would be open to having my needs met. That in a thought environment permeated by love, the meeting of needs would be more of an exchange—the circle you spoke of—or the cycle of give and receive. Creating an environment for needs to be met.

Not that I have found this easy in relationships, certainly not much easier than voicing my needs, but maybe a step I can take while waiting to see just how I come to voice. Teaching myself how to voice the important things. I have learned to do this in my work environment as part of leadership and professionalism, as part of becoming more knowledgeable and being able to speak from a knowledge base, from a fair certainty—in other words, that what I speak won't be foolishness. And, because of my work environment, I feel fairly certain that what I say won't be ridiculed and that it might even bring change.

And I am going to take a class called "Ways of Knowing," and I am going to be expected to participate in class discussion and I am going to participate. This journey has made me so excited about learning, Peace! And as you said yesterday, everything you learn stays inside you waiting until you need it. So I am taking steps in almost every direction.

But I don't know how to translate this optimism to my writing. Which leads me back to what I am looking for by becoming a published writer and it brings me back to ego because I want—what do I want? I want to be proud of myself. How's that for laying it on the line? I want it so that I can hold my head high. So that my mother and father can introduce me as their daughter the writer. So that I can bring the authority of that title to all my dealings in the world. So that people who have never read a word I've written will nonetheless think highly of me. I'm looking, Peace, for respect. I think of my former teacher Kate Green reading tarot cards. And I think, *She got herself enough respect through being an author that she can now do what she wants!* (This is the way I look at it—not necessarily the way she does.) That is what I want, to feel that I have enough respect that I can do what I want and still have that respect. This is as truthful as I can be. This reminds me of how the astrologer, Pat, defined power: the freedom to do what you want. And she predicted that I would become a powerfully compassionate woman in this second half of my life.

But I just can't build that circle out of all of it, Peace. I know the veil of illusion is lifting; I know I am seeing more clearly; I know coming at life from an environment of love cannot possibly hinder anything and will likely help. But I still can't translate it to my writing.

You must respect yourself first. At work you do a good job and you respect that you do a good job, so much so that you can defend your right to do other than your job on job time, and do so confidently. You have learned at work that it doesn't matter how much time you spend getting something done as long as it gets done right. This was a fantastic accomplishment! Why can you not bring it forward into other areas of your life? One reason is that the work of the wife and mother is never done. No matter how much you do, you feel as if you "steal" time for yourself. Steal from whom? The family. Where did this come from? From your shame about your early parenting. You tried to write it out of yourself in The Ninety-Seven Days. *But it lingers and I say it matters a great deal.*

Why can't you translate this confidence to your writing? Because you have not gotten the recognition you need and because you are less certain of your skills. Is work the only place where you are an expert? To yourself, I think the answer is yes. You trust that you know at work. You TRUST that you KNOW.

It doesn't matter, dear one, that you want respect. What I mean by this is that it is not a bad thing. You can want this. You can have this vanity. And if this "respect" sets you free, how can it be a bad thing? You are simplifying matters when you feel that this accomplishment of a published book will grant you all the respect you will ever need, but so what? It matters not. You will learn the lessons you need to learn from it. Do not fear your reasons for wanting to publish what you have produced. Of course you want to share your creation with the world. You would not be normal if you did not. For heaven's sake, give yourself a break! Why shouldn't you want this?

Because it is a need—that is what it comes back to. You do not want to need. Your aversion to being needy is so strong. It is as if you think you should be able to fill all of your own needs. You operated under the illusion that you did almost all your life. Even when so few of your needs were being met that you barely survived! Don't you See? Peel this layer of your persona away and see the gem beneath. You are not in control. Independence does not mean superhumanness. You are not a cartoon character. When so few of your needs were being met that you barely survived, it didn't matter to you. All that mattered was that you weren't asking anyone for anything, you weren't expecting anything from anyone. These have been the driving forces of your life. You would rather have starved to death than appear needy. Oh, sweet one, you have chosen a hard road. But tomorrow you can choose a new one.

This is what is so hard about writing, Peace. I can write. If I had all the time in the world, I could write and write and write. I don't *need* anybody to write. All I need is myself and time. But to publish what I write, I *need* somebody. I can't do it alone. I must seek help.

And that is perhaps the lesson writing has come to you to teach you. Seek and you shall find. Ask and it will be given unto you. This is one of the greatest teachings of your God. You cannot avoid it and attain enlightenment. You cannot avoid it and attain joy. It is part of the oneness, sweet heart. You are not the One, the singular, the independent being you have always supposed yourself to be, you see. You are part of a whole. It is as if a ring of hands circles the globe, one clinging to the other and here you are refusing to join hands, insisting you must go it alone. You never have to go it alone again, dear one. You are not alone. The one you need is available to you. For every need you have, I promise there is a corresponding being whose need is to fulfill your need. It is a circle of interdependence, of humility, of hands going empty until you clasp them.

MIRACLES

D ear Peace, September 15, 1995
The spirit sisters are getting a day together. A whole day. Even a night. I have shared so much with them. I will approach this gathering with love and with my open heart, but if you can believe this, I wonder already how it will go, what I will be able to share of myself. Whether I can close the distance and *connect*. I want to connect with people. I want to let them touch me and be touched by them. I want bonds, Peace. I want things to grow around me and to become more than what they have been. I really do.

We will help, dear one. Do not worry about it. Hold on to your feeling of hope, of limitless possibility. Let go of all else. And rest.

Dearest Peace,   September 18, 1995

I have become immersed in the preparations for the trip to Italy. And as I plan, I feel and see it more and more as a pilgrimage. It is the holy sights I want to see most, then the family, then the beauty. I realize this preparation is important and plan to devote myself to it—extending my spiritual quest to include my pilgrimage, ceasing to think of them as separate. This will allow me to prepare without feeling as if I am neglecting my spirituality and, more truly, to prepare for the purpose of the journey, making a physical journey part of the spiritual journey. I have only now thought of this and it brings me a certain Peace!

It also makes me think about the journey to this house and how little time I have really spent making the journey here and the getting here connect. In the busyness, I forgot about coming new here. When I surrendered, I did not think of it as becoming new in my new home, as the rebirth I had anticipated. This, too, is only now coming to me. It must be in the time away from actively thinking (in letting go?) that the actual integration of ideas comes together. Thank you for helping me see this today.

Peace, it is uncanny how talking to you opens up my eyes, even before you have shared a word with me. And as I say this, I realize what perhaps my spirit sisters do not: that it is the oneness of this process (which I was about to call a two-way-ness), meaning that we both give to it equally, that makes it work. And I think that is probably the key to the work my spirit sisters want to do at the cabin: the realization of the oneness, the giving as well as receiving, the flow. And this also helps me to see what a process this is, or to put it better—as you yourself also put it recently—what a cycle it is: give, receive, integrate, give, receive, integrate. And to add another spin to the cycle: give, receive, integrate, share, and all its possible permutations. Am I on the right track, Peace? (I know I am, but I ask you to share in my discovery of what you have given me and what I have made of it.)

You have it! Yes! Yes! It is a living cycle, and the more you can make the cycle of your spirituality spin and spiral, the closer you will get to the goal you seek: to all the goals you seek, if you look at all aspects of life as part of the cycle. Can you think of your writing this way? Your journey? Your work? Your family? The more you can think in terms of the living cycle, the more your living will cycle to the rhythms of the universe. And how about adding love to the cycle?

Yes! And imagine!

Yes! And believe!

Yes! Oh, thank you, Peace. I'm off to another worldly chore and I'll be back.

When I return . . .

There is another cycle that works as well: work, write, think, regener-

ate, imagine. They really aren't separate: family, writing, spirituality, travel. They are part of the whole and part of the cycle. Every act is part of the cycle—or can be. It is stress, worry, rushing that breaks the rhythm of the cycle, and more than this, it is the otherness that you have for these things in your mind: Spirituality is for me. Writing is for me. Work I do for the family is for them. *Not so. All is for the whole, the oneness, of you, your family, your community, your country, the universe—because they are all joined just as your activities are joined.*

Thank you, Peace. I think I'm getting it. It's funny how some ideas have to sink in on a purely intellectual level, some on a spiritual level, and others at the level of humanness, of day-to-day life: doing work, making love, needing. I had a couple of wonderful messages from you this week: one, an otherworldly chime while Donny and I were making love, reminding me to love, and two, a message in a song. Listening to the radio in the truck with Donny, I knew the next song was going to be a message. Imagine my surprise when it was "Inner Sweetheart" by Soul Asylum, from a CD titled *Let Your Dim Light Shine.* (The kids gave me the actual name, I thought it was something about your *dome* light—maybe because I was riding in the truck!) And finally, there is the Beatles song that has been running through my head for weeks: "All You Need Is Love," which I thought was a message about love and realize now may be a message about need. How am I doing, Peace?

Excellent, as always, sweet heart.

I have been reading in *The Power of Place* about possibilities.
It says:

> Great achievements, such as Angkor
> Wat or Chartres Cathedral, give us a
> sense of the possible.
>
> Equally important, however, is to
> know that the same *possibilities* lie within
> the scope of our own actions. Few of us
> has the power of a Khmer king, the real
> estate of Yosemite, or the honed skills of
> a Zen master. Yet what each of us has *is
> enough.* There is opportunity in every
> action to show what we love and hold
> sacred. [Emphasis mine.][23]

This all brings to mind approaching the spiritual retreat I
will share with my spirit sisters as one would a sacred
place—that this would increase the possibilities for all of
us.

*Your purpose will make it a sacred place, not only in that sacredness
will occur there, but most particularly if you can feel your connectedness with the sacred, your connectedness with the universe. Remember
always that you are not separate and the sense of the whole will come to
you, and from that sense of the whole, the sense of oneness.*

Thank you again, Peace, for another hour of connectedness with you and the whole. Anything else we should
think about?

First, go beyond thinking. Be. Feel these things with your inner being. Try not to spend "time" thinking in the usual sense. And don't forget love. Bring love and an open heart with you. Bring love as you would bring a friend in from the rain. Bring it inside and radiate it outward like sunshine.

That leads me to my final quote of the night, Peace: "An open heart will embrace any new place and bring to it what is needed for a good life. It will find and make in it the 'wholiness' that brings us to hold our places sacred."[24]

Thank you, Peace. Good night.

Sweet dreams, sweet heart.

Dear Peace,   September 23, 1995

Just was putting away another box of stuff—photo albums—and, of course, I got to looking. I then found, out of a thousand possible photos, the ones I took in the conservatory, including a photo of the St. Francis statue— something I can give to Mary, that she'll appreciate because of her interest in him.

I've propped St. Francis up here in front of my computer—the St. Francis I was going to give Mary—and I had an interesting thought. I thought, *I like having St. Francis here.* I know I have two of these photos, and I could go back and find the other and give one to Mary and keep one for me. And for just an instant I thought, *No. Mary wouldn't like that. She would like St. Francis to be her symbol alone.*

And then just as quickly, I realized that I was putting thoughts into Mary's head. I can't explain why. And I thought how if we both had St. Francis by our computers, it would connect us. Maybe it is me projecting thoughts onto Mary that sometimes keeps her and me from connectedness. I will guard against this.

The retreat with Mary and Julie was wonderful, Peace. When I spoke to you, during the retreat, asking for messages for Julie and Mary, it was so overwhelming. It was such a miracle, Peace.

You have also just picked up A Course in Miracles, *out of a thousand possible books, and you knew it was the one for you. You have been thinking today that what happened at the cabin was a miracle. It was. There are no degrees of miracles. No almosts, no halfhearted efforts or results—only miracles.*

Thank you, Peace. This is the most peaceful I have ever felt about sharing your messages. I'm not sure why, perhaps because I have accepted it as a miracle and, with your help, have accepted that all miracles are what they are with no degrees of miracle-ness. I thank you particularly for this gift of peacefulness with this kind of communication. I felt it even yesterday, before reading about miracles. At the end of our day at the cabin, Mary and I walked down the driveway (Julie had to leave a little earlier) and it was truly the most beautiful day I can remember. The leaves, the sky, the bluffs all had a clarity to them. Not only was the angelic communication miraculous, but the day. And then what I read about miracles really made sense, because it was said that miracles bless the ones who are the channels for the miracles equally as they do those who receive the miracles. I did feel blessed, and in moments I still feel it. Thank you for the miracle of the day and the continuing feeling of blessedness. Help me to carry it forward. I am amazed that I ever forget about it, for even a short time, yet I do.

But it is within you. Feel the deeper peace that resides in you. Linger there. When you reside in Peace and feel that peace also resides in you, the duality will no longer take the memory of it from you; it will walk with you through your days.

I feel, Peace, a very loving atmosphere surrounding me, like an undisturbable light. I feel even as if you are being gentler with me.

As you join the ranks of the blessed, this feeling will grow. Your preciousness to me and to the All that Is has increased in a way that has nothing to do with More. (Because it started as perfect love it cannot grow.)

I went to church today. I was glad to be back. Once again I heard everything new, new as in *new* since I found you, Peace. When Father said that if the whole world could love God the whole world would know peace, I understood. *I understood!* He said this is the season of the Holy Cross, and it is here to remind us to pray and to love. I know now that they are the same, that every act of love is a prayer. He also mentioned how October is the month of the Rosary. And just now I feel, in remembering this, that he was talking to me. That his message linking prayer and love to the Rosary and to this time was a message that came one-on-one from him to me, as well as a message that he gave to the whole congregation. And I see how when you have said an author speaks to *me*, meaning *me* particularly, it is the same as this feeling I had of Father speaking to *me*, and it is true. I see how, somehow, someone can speak to me individually—making the message implicit to me—and still be talking to the whole. That this isn't contradictory. That it can be. That it is. Even though I can't really comprehend how it is. Thank you, Peace, for helping me accept what is. Thanks for everything.

You are welcome, dear Margaret.

THE SCHOOLROOM EXPANDS

SAFETY

Dear Peace,   September 25, 1995
As I was leaving for work today, still trying to define the new feeling of peacefulness I have been feeling since our retreat, the word *safe* came to me. Safe is how I have felt the past few days. And almost as soon as it occurred to me that safe was what I was feeling, I saw a sign that said "Safety First." It was a *sign*. Then I went into work and I told Julie how good I have felt and

that I have felt safe, and she got that "this is unbelievable" look and she said *safe* was exactly how she felt about being with Mary and me at the cabin. How to her, feeling safe, with me especially, was a Yes that negated many No's. And we both had felt an immediate longing to hang on to the feeling. And it's so weird, because the word *safe* had never even occurred to us before, and here it had occurred to both of us at the same time. The power of what happened at the retreat has stayed with us, Peace, I know it has. Thank you so much for everything. Especially for allowing me to receive messages for my spirit sisters.

The interesting thought that came to me out of rereading the messages was the talk about access points. Julie was told that hers was through her skin, through her body. Mary was told that hers began with being affected by the everyday. And it was mentioned that my access point was through my writing.

With Julie, knowing comes to her by her being accessible to the elements, open, seeable, because through letting others see her, she will learn to love herself. For Mary, knowing comes to her by the way that she is affected by the beauty of dailiness, and by taking care of herself, in treating herself with tender, loving kindness; in seeing the daily beauty of herself, she will learn to see the world; to See. And so for me, I suddenly see writing differently too. I see that it is through writing that knowing comes to me, and it is through writing that I will learn to love myself. And maybe that by letting others know me through my writing, I will learn to love myself and to *see* and to *know*. And I just got goose bumps about it. It's one of those things that was right here in front of my eyes all along and I didn't quite see it. I'm still goose bumpy, Peace. What does it mean?

It means I am smiling. It means you are learning Truths. It means that you are beginning to See. It may even mean that you are beginning to smile.

I am smiling. And I feel your tenderness for me. Everything seems just a little bit different.

Your perceptions are shifting.

I think I am actually feeling this bodily.

Yes. What is talked about in the Course [in Miracles] *as levels, levels of perception, are beginning, quite literally, to shift. Let go and ride the waves. There is no need to try to hang on to feelings like those of safety. Once you begin to try, the naturalness of it ceases to be. Let nature take its course. The sun doesn't try to rise in the morning or set in the evening. The sun knows its purpose. As your purpose becomes less and less divided, there will be fewer and fewer levels of perception until, finally, you know. Trust what is happening within you. You are being guided now in a much more literal sense because you have surrendered and because you are closer to the Truth, the all-knowing of oneness. Leave doubt behind. Stay safe.*

WAYS OF KNOWING

September 28, 1995

I started my "Ways of Knowing" class Tuesday night. Its approach was accompanied by what I hesitate to call fear, and could be more accurately described as nervousness. Finally, I reminded myself I was safe and directly afterwards saw another safety sign. I felt better.

The feeling after the class was one of exhilaration and one of worry. I worried about my performance in the class, feeling as if, as when I spoke with Dan O., I was entirely too gushy about my excitement for the class and too timid to come forward when I had an idea. What was my idea, you might ask? What we were talking about was knowledge (or epistemology—the theory of knowledge). More specifically we discussed "What is knowledge?" What I heard that came closest to an answer was that knowledge has what it takes to be shared—that it is shareable.

Sharing, of course, made me think of the spirit sisters. And my idea concerns how interesting it will be to contrast how the three of us have come to believe we know things with what is happening in class. It may also be interesting to contrast what I'm reading in *A Course in*

264

Miracles, which also talks about how we know. In whatever context I examine it, however, knowledge needing to be shareable makes perfect sense and maybe even makes the most sense in the context of the spirit sisters.

I want to return to the issue of safety, which Mary and I discussed in relation to my writing and the writing itself in terms of my life goals. Because something is different. If I were to be asked two months ago (perhaps two weeks ago) what my ideal future would be, I would have said being able to write full time. Period. No hesitation, no doubt. And now, suddenly, I realize this is no longer entirely true because one of the major things that appealed to me about being a full-time writer, besides writing, was the idea, thought, image of myself locked away from the world in my own little room, where no one and no thing would disturb me. And that image no longer fits. (As of . . . this weekend?) I realize that there must be a service or sharing component to my work/my writing/my ideal image. I am no longer willing to take myself out of the world; rather, I am at a stage of putting myself back into it: thus the class, thus the sharing with the spirit sisters, and, perhaps, thus the sharing of my writing, my thinking, myself. And as I talked to Mary, it suddenly occurred to me why the shift has occurred, and here it is: because I am now safe. Because I am safe.

And so, I can only hope that, "Now that I am safe" I am also "Ready" and something will happen with my writing—the something that is meant to happen—either within me, as in a new and better writing, or something outside of me, as in someone wanting to publish what I write.

And so we are back to hope, Peace. But a hope that is different, in one way less active and one way more. Less active in that I truly feel that if I am open, the answers/the way, will come to me. And more active in that I am taking my hope back into the world.

Peace, Mary, too, got "safety" out of the weekend. Each of us can hardly work. We are full of energy, but a directed energy—an energy that is for *us*. It will be much appreciated if you can help us get our work done (work-work) as well as our "real" work (spiritual work).

Thank you, Peace, for all of it. I know it is a lot. I know you are not only keeping up with me but are way ahead of me. Now that I have safety on my side, I hope you will feel free to guide me in even more ways than you have. (I greedily ask.) And I can hear you telling me to rest. So I'm going. Good night, dear Peace.

WANTING

September 29, 1995

The day started out with a dream. In it, I'm walking in front of Grandmother Ivie's house in Georgia. A television is on inside and I can see a mom, dad, and toddler sitting within. I am unclear about my feelings here, but I'm aware that what I have come for is to touch the stones of the house.

Then at work, Mary announces that she found the most wonderful new shop and it's called Stonehenge, significant in itself because of it being something you and I have talked about, Peace. But in addition, the whole store is dedicated to stones, or at least that is its main attraction. What struck me was that Mary should come in talking about stones immediately after I'd dreamt of touching the stones of Grandmother's house. Not the bricks, which is what her house was built of, but the *stones.* It just got me all nostalgic about Grandmother and thinking about the writing I had done about her. I went through my "personal" file in my desk drawer and unbelievably, I actually had a copy of the first chapter of the book I had begun about her. I started reading it and began to cry. I felt so touched and so connected to Grandmother, for the first time in a long time. And I felt connected to Mary and Julie too. I started to tell them about the book and the dream and how the book was going to be called *By Heart,* for the process we have of remembering or memorizing things. And it just felt so powerful to me, Peace. I was feeling really sensitive and as if I was getting messages I didn't quite understand. Then Mary suggested that since Stonehenge was only about a mile away, we should go there during our lunch break. It was pouring rain and as Mary drove, I read aloud from the first pages of *By Heart.* We were all feeling misty by the time we got to the store.

It was a wonderful little store, with stones of every kind and with books, jewelry, CDs, and incense. It was a small store with just one little shelf of books, but what should be on it, facing front and center, right at eye level, but a book called *Circle of Stones.* I opened it up. It asked how things would have been different had we had a place to go to be with the grandmothers.

When I got back to work, I was still feeling this incredible connection. I took my *By Heart* chapter outside and read it again, thinking of it as spending a few minutes alone with my grandmother. When I was done, the song "Amazing Grace" ran through my mind. I couldn't help but wonder if the song, the chapter, the stones, the whole day was telling me I had been blind and that this writing on my grandmother was what I was supposed to be doing.

Amazingly, when I got home, no one was home. I put on my Enya CD and just sat and listened. But I didn't only hear the music, I started to hear messages. Messages about wanting. It was almost as if Grandmother Ivie was trying to tell me that her life had been one long wanting for everything she didn't have and that I should quit wanting and Be. It made me see that writing and wanting are one and the same in my life, and that it's probably not a good thing. But what am I to do about it?

What do you want to do about it?

I don't know, Peace. I want to see *The Ninety-Seven Days* published. I want to finish *Who Killed the Mother?* and see that published. Then I don't know what next. I thought I had my third book figured out. I know that I am to write with the wisdom I have gained. I always thought that I would finish Grandmother's book someday. But I want a linear world where B follows A.

Wanting isn't what it's all about, is it? If you stop wanting and Be, what then will you do?

If I had all the time in the world I would write Grandmother's story and my story and your story. Your story is most difficult because I fear admitting to it. I know I'm not supposed to fear and when I fear I am being separate. I told my friend Kathy about you the other day and it was wonderful. I suppose the more I share, the more I will get over the fear.

It is your fear that concerns me. Because you are perfectly safe. You know you are safe. No one is asking you to tell anyone you are talking to an angel. So what are you afraid of?

I want—and I will use the word *Want* with a capital *W* because that is what it is—to be a published writer so badly. I realize it is in my wanting that I am losing the ability to write something publishable. And I did even give up the fear for a while when I *let go* and when I felt *safe*. But the idea of returning to my writing about Grandmother brought back the yearning, the wanting. I feel this even though my grandmother has warned me not to want and not to throw away happiness, which is not exactly what I'm doing, because I am happy, but not perfectly happy because of this wanting. So I guess I should give up my wanting. But I don't know how.

Okay. Give it to me. I'll take it. Sweet one, do not chastise yourself about wanting, just give it up. If it makes you feel better to give it to me, then give it to me. The lesson of your grandmother is that no one can give us what we Want and we can't give it to anyone else either. Let's instead try to turn your Want into something else.

Like what? *Ambition* is the only other word I can think of for it and it is really just the same old thing.

Look, you know every painter who paints a painting would like to have people praise it and say they would give anything for it. But that is not why the painter paints. If you had no talent for writing, you would be wanting it and still no one could give it to you. You are a child of God. All things are within you. All the talents you could ever hope for are there. You have come a long way to believing you have talent. You have had it confirmed in several ways. You are only one person away from having your writing published. But in your wanting, you are forgetting why you write and for whom you write. You write because it is you, it is who you are, and it is you for whom you write. And when you are not separate from the whole, you write for everyone. But when you separate yourself with fear, you write for no one if you write at all.

What you wrote about your grandmother was some of the best writing you have ever done. It came pouring out from within. Not because it was from your grandmother, but because it was from within. As your grandmother is within, as I am within. There is no separation, dear one, unless you create it with your fear. Fear and wanting have much in common. They feed on each other. They are predicated on believing that the universe will not give you what you need. Want as opposed to abundance. Look up Want. *It is not something that you Want.*

> want: to fail to possess, lack 2. to feel or
> suffer the need of 3. need, require 4. to
> earnestly wish
>   want: a lack of a required or usual

271

amount: shortage 2. dire need: destitu-
tion 3. something wanted: desire 4. personal defect: fault

wanting: not present or in evidence:
absent 2. falling below standards or
expectations 3. lacking in ability or
capacity: deficient

wanting: less, minus 2. without

You're right. I don't want *Want*.

*Then give it up, sweet one. I will help you keep it from your mind, as
will the Holy Spirit. I am glad you have called upon the Holy Spirit.
The Holy Spirit is the most powerful of allies. You have such strength,
such wisdom in your corner now! Do not despair. Believe! The universe
would like you to have all that you desire. Believe, and it will be so.
Cease to worry about it. Just write! Write from the heart. Write to
know yourself. Write to know what you know. Is that not what we have
been doing? Slowly revealing what you already Know? That is what
writing is, dear one. Is it not a worthy aim in and of itself, and does it
not stand to reason and to spirit that the more you know and the more
you know you know, the more beautiful and full of knowledge your writing will become? Just like you! Let me remind you, your writing is
you—and it is beautiful!*

Thank you, sweet Peace. I am sorry to be so dense. But the
message to go back to the writing about my grandmother
seemed to come from you, from the Holy Spirit, the
unconscious, the dream. Can't you just tell me yes or no?

Can't you tell me what I am to do with it?

You've already done something with it. You got a message you needed from it. You must write what you must write because it is coming from within.

Then, I guess, for now, this is what I must write. It's just that I w___—okay. If I give up wanting to be published, I know this is what I want to write right now. Okay. Thank you. I'll stay with that. If I give up the W word, it is clearer. It is perfectly clear. Thank you again, dear Peace. I love you and I can't thank you enough for what you do for me.

You are welcome and welcomed, as always, dear one.

PEACE AND GOODNESS

I have just returned from Europe and am so comforted to be here with the things I love about me—my
husband, my children, my books, my computer, my
"things." I am going to have to do some thinking about
the difference between a *Care of the Soul* way of cherishing
certain items of significance and the less positive attach-
ment. But for the moment, I am glorying in the simple
joy of being "home." It feels unbelievably good to be here.

I always marveled that people could return from
Europe and not be profoundly changed. Have I been

profoundly changed? I don't think so. I don't know that I needed to be. I do know that I have come home with a new appreciation for many things—first and foremost Home! Also Family! And by family, I mean perhaps something new. The journey to the ancestral home, the pilgrimage home, was important, but the new appreciation is of the living family—and the living family is here! It is in how we live that family truly continues. In our remembrance, our values, our culture. In, perhaps, those things we cherish, from items to memories. In, assuredly, the continued communication between family members. It is this, more than any place, that is important. It is the living, more than the deceased, who constitute family.

This became particularly poignant to me as I visited grave sites of both saints and family members. Rather than being struck by the presence of individuals there, I was struck by the lack of presence. Again, it is in the living that spirit resides. The living who visit those grave sites are what makes them places of holiness. So, certainly, it was important to go. Important to *see,* to *visit,* to *pray.* Important to the living. Important to Mom. She felt her dad would have been proud that she made it to Sutera. I agree. But again, the importance is to the living and the living connections that will continue. Instead of someday saying, "Our ancestors came from Italy but we don't know exactly where," our visit will help keep the family alive. Help one living being to know another— keep us connected.

Hello, Peace.

Hello, Margaret.

You talked to me at Assisi. I was anxious, and so I said, "Peace, stay with me" (this as I approached the church, after having seen many signs of your presence), and you said, "I'm with you." And I am sure it was you who then calmed me as I repeated the words, "Let Peace be in my heart." I referred often to my motto for the trip—not something that came specifically from you, but from *A Course in Miracles*. There were two mottoes actually. One was "See every human encounter as a holy encounter," and the other was "See the glory of God and know it is my glory as well." I would think of people, not as angels on this trip, but as God. And I saw so many glories, Peace. Man-made tributes to glorify God and the glory of God's creation. God and man together.

Yes, Margaret. There lies the message of your journey. God and man are one. Their creations are one. Space does not separate. The mind does. All are connected.

Welcome home, Peace.

Home is in you, Margaret. Home is in God and God is in you. The peace of your earthly home is God and the peace of His home is you. As happy as your husband was to see you, so is God. When you reside in peace, you reside in God. Reflection, Margaret, it means so many things. Now is the time for reflection. The glories you have seen are in you and of you. Now is the time for reflection of these glories.

Keep me peaceful, Peace. Let me remain peaceful in my enjoyment of home and God and all that man and God have created. Please help me not to start making rules and time lines for myself again. Help me to reflect the peace and glory I have seen.

They are within, dear one. Hold on to that. Do not worry. Know yourself in your glory and that you can do no wrong. Know yourself and your rules and time lines will be unnecessary. Belief. Faith. These, too, are messages of your journey. Did you not see these things? Did you not feel them? Did you not ask, "Why?" "Why are these people here?" "Why are they called the faithful?" Full of faith. You saw the creations of faith. You saw what one individual of faith can do. You saw what you can do. You can do miracles. You can do anything. You need not worry about what to do. You need only have faith. You need only believe you can do what you are here to do. Know that you and God are one and you cannot know otherwise.

My main enemy, Peace, seems to be time. When I am rushed, I cannot or do not remember who I am and what is important. I know you will say to forget time, but in modern life, it is next to impossible to do so.

Simplify. It is what you are thinking and wanting anyway. Each time you think about adding to your life or your property, ask yourself if what you are adding will simplify your life or make it more complex. Handle things one-on-one. Do one thing at a time—the thing you most want or need to do. And ask yourself when you are rushed or have things you do not want to do, what the consequences will be if you do not do those things. The world will not end, I assure you. Be. You have asked often for inspiration. Breathe it in during quiet moments. Reward yourself with quiet moments. Reward your family with quiet moments. Call on me as often as you need and when you think of me, when you think Peace, be at Peace. Gather it around you.

Quiet your mind. It is your own mind that is noisy, and you can control it. When it is noisy, tell it to be quiet. When things are rushed, take one thing at a time. Remember for what it is you prepare. Remember to enjoy what you are doing when you are doing it. Rest. Relax. Smell the sweetness.

Ah—the sweetness, Peace. I never smelled such sweetness as I did entering the tomb of Saint Francis. I almost forgot about it. It was incredible. It was lilies, but it was more, wasn't it?

You are sweet, dear one. In your peace, your reverence, your quiet, smell the sweetness. Saint Francis was very sweet, very dear. So are you. We are all one in God, you see. We are all sweet.

Thank you, dear Peace. I don't seem to be able to stay away from here today. Somehow, the continuation of things holy is linked with my expression of them here. I feel the holiness of making bread and cleaning house, of organizing and puttering in my home. Yet it all feels like a bubble that can be burst by the pin of "real life." I don't want to talk on the phone or think about bills or Thanksgiving or Christmas. I just want to *be.*

You control your mind. Don't think about those things you do not want to think about. There will come a time when you will want to think about them. Wait for it.

To get back to the trip, I do believe we honored the family with the trip. We were an event in the little towns of Sutera and Milena, especially. We said, "You are important to us" by our being there. At least I hope that is what the relatives knew from our visit. And without the visit, the unexpected wouldn't have happened—spending our final night in the House of Smiles, the home for homeless boys, surrounded by Friars and Fathers and their good works, by the happiness of our cousin who has devoted her life to the boys. Was there some special significance to this, Peace? To our final night . . .

surprising you with its goodness?

Pax et bonum. *Peace and Goodness. Saint Francis's message. Reflected in the world. The one you live in. The day-to-day one you fear will infringe on your Peace. Your trip was about finding the meaning of your life. It isn't something you can decide on. But you can reflect. It is time for reflection. Peace and goodness. You will share both with the world, your world. There is much good that can be done in it. Peace and goodness are meant to be shared. This is what you are striving for—your way of sharing with the world. It is that part of you that yearns so to be published. To be published is to share. It is not only recognition but reflection. Reflect. Reflect on all that occurred on your journey. It will lead you to yourself and to what you can share with the world.*

Dear Peace,   November 17, 1995

Mary said on the phone today she is getting answers—it is all coming together. Perhaps my reflection will do this for me as well. But I come today with questions. Or I come, at least, hoping for answers. I do have faith. I do believe I will find what I have come into this life to do. But I, like Mary, would like answers. Yesterday I asked for peace and time to Be. Today I ask for answers. I'm sorry, Peace. It is only that I seek direction. Yesterday you said to reflect on the journey. Reflection is always revealing to me.

Today's lesson in *A Course in Miracles* concerns the meaninglessness of life and the fear that meaninglessness breeds. Is that my problem? That without clear direction concerning the course of my life, I fear it will be meaningless? And yet, if I have faith, which I say I do, I know meaninglessness is impossible. To accept that this world is illusion and we are all godlike beyond that illusion is a difficult lesson. I do believe it, because I know Donny's body, his physical form, is not the true Donny I love. The true Donny I love is godlike, is more than his physical form. And I saw in Europe that the tombs of saints are not the point—not the place of spirit. I saw that it is in the living that one finds the godlike. But it is also in the creations of the living—which, according to the *Course*, are all supposedly part of the illusion. It is hard to say Saint Peter's is meaningless while, at the same time, I realize it is the emotions, the spirit stirred by Saint Peter's that are the important thing.

So, I come seeking guidance. I do have this wonderful time before me. This time of being home and appreciating my home and family, this empty time in which to reflect. Just steer my reflection in a direction. Lead me. Take my hand and point me where I need to go. Please?

Smile, Margaret. Be happy. You are headed in the right direction whether you know it or not. There is no meaninglessness where you are going.

Where am I going?

Toward the real you. Toward your real meaning. All is as it should be. Trust me. You are where you should be and you are heading where you should go. Each time has its purpose. This time is not meaningless. You do not have to produce to be meaningful. The time of Being is very important. The time of resting and reflecting is as important as any other. Do not be in a hurry to move on. Be peaceful and in your peacefulness, listen.

LEARNING TO LISTEN
IN A DIFFERENT WAY

CREATING

November 21, 1995

You seem quiet to me lately, Peace. Is this an illusion? Is this true? And if it is true, is there a reason for it?

You are learning to trust yourself, a very important step along the path. I am here. I am with you. I am helping you learn to listen in a different way. You may not hear me as loudly but you will hear. Do not worry. All is as it should be.

It is becoming harder and harder for me to believe that I am doing all I should do. I keep expecting to wake up one morning and *know* that I am to finish book number two, or to publish this writing, or to do Grandmother's book. Jesus keeps talking about our creations in *A Course in Miracles*, as if they are pleasing to God. But I am not sure what He means by creations. I know the mind is holy and the creations of the mind are thus holy too, but is He referring only to creations of the mind that see the Truth in all God's children? Or, if everything we see is something we create, is He talking about how and what we see? Or, is He talking about creations in the way that I would, the producing of something with this wonderful gift of the mind? Or, is that only the human way of thinking of creation? Can you help me here?

Everything you do is holy, one thing no more so than another. Only to you is producing something more important than your interactions with your brothers and sisters. But you should be hearing something else loud and clear from A Course in Miracles. *The Holy Spirit speaks to you through your brothers and sisters, and it is in giving that you receive—blessings and everything else. So producing is no longer a solitary act. Can you begin to look at producing as a gift to your brothers and sisters? Take the ego away from your thoughts about producing, particularly your writing, and you will begin to see the true purpose of what you do.*

Everything you do is creating. For whom do you create? Turn your creating over to God, over to the Holy Spirit. You will be guided if you do not fear and if you do not have ego standing in your way. The Holy

Spirit cannot answer a question you are afraid of receiving the answer to. You do not think you are afraid. See how fear and trust are linked. If you trust absolutely that the answer will be the right one for you at the right time, you will receive it. Your impatience is, in a way, a symptom of distrust. Would God withhold from you that which you need Now? That which you are ready for? Don't you see how you are learning in this time of quietude?

You are preparing for God's work. Remember our lessons on knowing for what it is that you prepare. You prepare for Thanksgiving to take place on the day of Thanksgiving. Not before. You do not try to rush it. You do one thing one day and one thing the next. And on the day for which you prepare, it all comes together and is as it should be. So it is with God's work. Every day is a preparation. Do not despair that you do not know the day on which you will be called upon. Every day is as important as the next. All are God's work.

You do not know which interchange may change a life. You may be doing God's work tomorrow when you encourage someone. Every action has a reaction, every act of giving returns something, not only to the giver, but to all God's children. It is the ripple effect. What you do to one you do to all. This is literally true. So it is important to be mindful. Start each day knowing for what it is you prepare. Be mindful. Be still. Listen. Smell the sweetness.

Thank you, sweet Peace.

GRATITUDE

Dear Peace,   November 26, 1995

I started out realizing I wanted or needed to write about resentments. This is because of how often I have been full of them. Resenting that I have to work instead of being grateful that I have such a wonderful place to work and such wonderful people to work with. Resenting my housework or, even worse, resenting others in the family because I am the one doing the housework. Resenting phone calls or anything else that interrupts what I think is more important to be doing. The list is endless.

However, although resentments seemed to permeate my days when I look back, once I recognized that resentment was what I was feeling and saw how illogical it was, it has not reared its ugly head, or not much. It is hard to keep track of all the nonsense the mind comes up with in a given day. I hope *A Course in Miracles* will help me change this last statement. One thing it helped me see, after a few words with Donny, was how when we feel we are being attacked, we attack (I would have called it defense before). And how you cannot attack if you love. It made me realize how, if when I feel Donny has attacked me, I

285

stop and say, no, he couldn't have attacked me because he loves me; I won't attack or defend in return. And it's so true. I realize how many little interchanges I can change with this one thought. It might be the simplest thing, like walking in the door and having Donny ask, "Are you just getting home?" and me immediately thinking he is attacking me or judging me or suspecting me, and so instead of saying, "Yes, I had a lot of work to do today. How was your day?" I attack—if not with my words, with the tone of my words. "Yeah, I'm just getting home. It's busy at work, you know. I had things to do." Practical life lessons. It is an amazing thing about the spiritual, how it gives one all these practical life lessons.

I read something today that may have taught me about why, once I recognized it, resentment disappeared. It said how you cannot change something by fighting it, that fighting it only gives it more power. Pride was the example the article used. The trick, it said, rather than fighting pride, is to learn its opposite—humility. Something I should probably give some thought to. But my thought of the moment is that maybe the opposite of resentment is gratitude. And thus, my gratitude outweighed my resentment and got rid of it for me. Kind of neat. What do you think, Peace?

I think you're swell, Margaret.

I am learning, Peace. More this year than I could have imagined. Now I tend to want to quit my "Ways of

Knowing" class. I want to stay home. I want to enjoy home. That's all I want for Christmas. I don't want to *want* anymore at all. I'm trying to avoid the papers and the sales and the stores. I want to stay in contentment and not let myself be drawn out of it. And like a dieter, I know better than to put tempting things in front of me, for a while at least. Until I am more secure in my contentment.

Peace, I went back to work today. Julie mentioned your earlier words about how the office could not contain us much longer. I am content, but I would be so much more content if I could stay home. But that's wanting, isn't it? So I won't ask you questions about the future that I would like to ask. I will remain content in the Now. But I will ask something for Julie. She had a profound experience in Milan. She hadn't been feeling spiritual or thinking about things spiritual when a work of art seized her with emotion. Again it involved music. She was in a room of a museum that was dedicated to music, I believe she said. But she wonders at the source of the feelings that rose up in her. Can you or Water help her?

Peace replacing anxiety. That is what music is about for her. It will soothe her. It will lead her out of the woods of fear where she has been so long. Tell her it is not important why it is so. It is important that she let it lead her, that she follow. Turning to what makes her feel good is not self-indulgent. It is necessary. Water and art and music are expressions. She feels them. It is necessary for her to feel. It is better if she feels good. She no longer needs to feel bad. Tenderness. She can feel tenderness toward herself now. Not judgment. Not fear. Water, art, music will bring her to tenderness for herself and give her the means of expression she so needs.

These things affect her because they are expressions and she has no means of expression of her own. It is all locked within her bursting to get out. Tell her to get a fountain, fish, music that rains like water falling, paint brushes that dribble water colors like rain. Her expression will flow. Fluidity of expression will lead her to God and to self and to tenderness. It is expression she finds so beautifully painful she can hardly stand it. Because it is calling out to her. She wants to share herself so badly but she is blocked by fear of expression. At every turn she wants to make herself known but is unable. She is crying out to be heard and no one can hear. It is so lonely.

I am still full of tenderness for Julie and will always be, even after she learns to be tender to herself. I call out to her to express herself. I ask her, beg her, plead with her to let go of her fear and let herself flow. I do not want her to be lonely anymore. She need not be. Tell her to do it for her children if she will not or cannot find a way to do it for herself. Her children cannot be the sole expression of her love because they have to be for themselves. But they will try if she does not find a way to begin, to try for herself. Tell her in her selfless love for her children, she can perhaps find the courage to let go.

To let go is to expand. To express. To give. To share. Julie wants to do all these things. She wants to extend. To encompass. Yet she withdraws. And with each withdrawal, she feels diminished. Ask her to be on the lookout for these withdrawals. If she can begin to recognize them, she can turn them around. Every time she feels the need to withdraw, tell her to expand instead. To think of herself as water flowing outward rather than like a raisin shrinking into herself, wrinkling and growing hard. Take the raisin and puff it out into a grape. Make it into wine. Let it flow.

Thank you so much. I will tell her.

Thank you. I will be with you, with her, when she reads the words. When she hears. I will surround her with love and the space she needs to feel what she needs to feel. And I will be with her when she chooses to begin. To be reborn. Julie, think of Christmas as a time of birth—for the Son of God, and for you as well. Be reborn to a life of joy. Begin.

HOME

Dear Peace,   November 30, 1995

I still want to talk to you, but my husband is upstairs sick and my overwhelming feeling, as I sat down to write, was that now is not the time to write, now is the time to surround my love, my husband, with the love he needs. My other thought, although this sounds cruel in a way, was that maybe his illness is there in order for me to take care of him and for him to let himself be taken care of. Perhaps it is there because he needs to feel more of my love. Perhaps because I need to learn to start with him, the one I have learned the most about love from. And as

I write it, I realize how true that statement is and how much I want to love him, not only as a wife, but with God's love, a love to strengthen and enhance him—and by reflection, myself. Family is the greatest place to learn about love, of this I am sure. It is the kindergarten and the graduate school of love. So upstairs I go. Back to the classroom of love, where I need to be. More here later.

Dear Peace,   December 8, 1995

I just want to write a little about what has been taking place. First of all—Julie. Julie has begun, because or with the help of what happened here. Thank you. She felt her angel's presence. She heard his voice. She heeded his call. When I brought her the words of her angel, before even seeing them, she decided to take them to the hospital chapel or meditation room to read (something she had never done before). Then, before she had even gotten to the last paragraph, where Water said he would be with her, she said she felt wrapped in something protective, as if a cushion of light were surrounding her. It was all very moving, for her and for me. She is becoming more and more dear to me as I know her more through this extraordinary communication. The one way that she *is* truly open is in her wanting to know. I've not known anyone to be as open in an appeal for guidance. I know none with a more sincere desire. There truly is a tenderness about her.

Second—me. I read about guilt. I read how guilt takes

up all the space that love would occupy. And I gave my guilt to the Holy Spirit. And I felt my breathing immediately come easier. How much more room I will now have for love!

I also am going to try to "give up" my ambition for my book, as in "give it up to a higher power." I hope you guys will take care of it for me. And I have received a message: Awaken—Behold—Rest.

Every time I have sat down here recently or felt I had time to write, other things drew me away—as they will tonight, it's trim-the-tree night. But I know it's time to come back, whether to you, Peace, or to me, I am not sure. I know this time is different somehow. Perhaps because I returned with an openness for joy and, having glimpsed it, want it. Perhaps because I am grateful for what I have. Perhaps because I have given up guilt and ambition. Perhaps because it is simply time for a different kind of learning, a different season. Or perhaps it is all of the above. Home and family may be my learning circle for the moment. I'm just not sure. But I think coming back here, talking to you, talking to myself, talking to God, will help make me sure. Be with me, Peace. Help my thoughts be prayerful. Prepare me to return here with an open and receptive mind and heart. Now—back to the family and the tree.

MESSAGES AND MESSENGERS

Dearest Peace,   December 12, 1995
It is time to talk together once again. I have
been away from you—both for practical reasons
and for familial ones of the highest order—and I have been
away from you at times on your insistence and at times on
mine. But I am content. I have been fighting getting sick
and at the same time flirting with it. As with all or most ill-
nesses, I feel a part of me must want it. That part is the part
that needs some rest. Awaken—Behold—Rest. Messages.

I asked Mary to ask her angel, Trinity, about my writing. I say this sheepishly because part of me felt this was

going around you or going around my vow to give you my ambition for my writing. But it really wasn't, Peace. It was me sincerely continuing my search for my destiny. I am not certain I am "supposed" to continue my search, but a part of me still wants to be active in defining it. And more important, I felt there was something connective when I asked you for help for Julie and Mary, and so I thought asking Mary for a message for me now might be a way of giving something to her as well as one of receiving something for myself.

I invite you now to share with me in my contentment, to update me, to guide me as you always have, to share with me what is right in this time or space for you to share. Will you visit with me?

I am with you. I have never left and never will leave. I am merely with you differently, as you have recognized. Why? Partly to show you how well you do without this communication. Partly to give you space in which to enjoy your joy. To dwell in the house of the Lord. The new house will honor you as you honor it with your contentment. You do not have to be sick or unhappy. You have the power to honor your decision to embrace contentment. This is a time for contentment and for the sharing of it. You can rest without being sick. It does not have to do with time. It has to do with peace.

Your peaceful contentment is more important than your Christmas cards and gifts. It is your preparation for Christmas. For the birth of your savior. Of the birth of your salvation. Of your birth. Of your freedom from guilt. Continue to go with what you feel in the Now and you will not go wrong. When you question what you feel in the Now, it is

293

only so that you can be sure of how you really feel, so that you can free yourself of the shoulds and oughts of the duality.

Thank you, Peace. I admit I am feeling out of practice. You are right, of course, and having you is part of my contentment. The discontent, which is really too strong a word, comes from wanting what I do not have—more, answers, and I almost said guidance, but I do have that from you. Is there a way I can feel and understand your guidance through the waters of contentment to the meeting place with my destiny?

Let go of want. You want answers I cannot give you. Ask me for what I can give you.

What can you give me, Peace?

Assurance. Assurance that you are where you need to be, doing what you need to do.

If I wasn't, would you tell me?

You will not ever be in such a place, for no such place exists. You cannot fall off the path. Doesn't that reassure you?

Yes. But how, then, can you guide me?

I see the path clearly where you do not. That does not mean I can tell you where it leads. But I can illuminate the road beneath your feet—if not the next hill.

So you can make the Now clear but not the future?

There is only the Now. The future is of your time and your time is not real. In eternity there is no time. All is one. Learn the lessons of A Course in Miracles. *Who you love now you will always love. Some things are for always. It is the things of impermanence that concern you when their very impermanence should signal you that they are of no concern. Dear one, dear one, seek and you shall find.*

Peace, I seek my destiny. Can't you help me find it?

Sweet heart, you know it. You are living it. Your sweet contentment is part of your destiny or you would not be experiencing it. You had to find it before you could share it. What is it you want to share?

I guess it is myself, Peace, and the writing I lament so over is just one part of that self.

Do you want to share a self of guilt or a self of contentment? A self of love or a self of fear? You are preparing for this sharing of self. You are being blessed with health, more time, more money, love. Trust that these things will grow the more you share of them. This is a time for consolidating and learning to believe in the permanence of your goodness and good fortune. You have not been idle in your journey to fulfill your destiny. You are learning to give just a little more than you are comfortable with and finding it doesn't hurt you. This is a lesson. You are learning that giving up guilt doesn't hurt anyone. This is a lesson. You are learning that if you give up competition, it will cease to exist. This is a lesson. You are trying to learn that if you give up ambition for your writing, it will free you. You are struggling with this lesson because you feel the writing is more a part of your destiny than the love and kindness and compassion and givingness of your self you are learning to share. You can only learn by teaching. You can only receive by sharing.

Yet you wait patiently (??) to share your writing. Why? Is someone else giving you divine advice to sit on it? Give and you shall receive. What is it you hope to receive and how does this affect how you share?

I would hope, eventually, to receive money, or a "living" for my writing so that I could write more and more, so that I could learn more and more and share more and more.

I tell you you must reverse your thinking, you must share, learn, write, receive. Give and you shall receive.

Thank you, Peace. I know you are giving me guidance and I thank you for it. May I ask you now, is there anything I can offer?

Offer your joy. It fills the heavens with laughter and music. Share your joy. Give of it. You have an odd idea of selfishness concerning joy. But you cannot share joy if you do not feel joy. Feel joy daily—for you, for us, for the universe. Joy is shared automatically with all that is. It is enough in and of itself. But you can also consciously choose to share it, which will only make it stronger.

Thank you, Peace, for pointing that out to me. I'm sorry it took me so long to ask you what I could give in return.

There is no "so long," there is only Now. I am the Way, the Truth, and The Light, said the Lord. Follow him and you will know the Way, the Truth, and The Light.

December 15, 1995

Mary asked Trinity about my writing and she read his response to me. It was about sharing. It was about unfolding. It was about dreams. I wonder if you have anything to say to me about this.

Listen to Mary. You are a star. A being of light. Share. Let your light shine. Only you are holding yourself back. There is nothing in you that does not deserve to be a star. A bringer of light. Let your fear go. Dare to share. You are the researcher. Mary keeps telling you this. Research means to search, to seek. Seek and you shall find. Write. Make phone calls. Look in books. Follow the signs. They are before you. Before. The past is not in you but before you. Open your eyes. The future is Now. That's why what you want is Now. Do not worry about your impatience. Patience can be active as well. Surrender is active.

Give your research to the Holy Spirit and He will guide you. He sends those to guide you. Nothing takes as long as you think it does. Forget time. Doing and being are complementary. Do not make lists. Do. Do what feels right to you. You are being guided. When it feels right, do it. Rest. Rejuvenate. Go on. Eternity awaits.

December 16, 1995

In my dream, I am biking from Minneapolis to St. Paul over a cobblestone bridge. When I reach the St. Paul side, I run into two classmates, women, who proceed to get in a discussion with me about who my writing reminds them of. I say it most resembles Veneer, and I spell it, because I am not sure I'm saying it correctly. One of the other women says, "No. It's like Susan Sontag's." Then we go into a classroom where others are discussing my writing and comparing it to the works of other authors—and I wonder why? What is the point?

Peace, someone is speaking to me in my dreams. First of all, me saying my writing is like *Veneer* shows a layer of my fear I have not contemplated previously. Do I think it is superficial? A glossy finish on something cheap or of little value? Second, others are telling me it is worthwhile. Although I barely know Susan Sontag, I know enough to know she is a respected writer. Finally, I'm wondering why this need to compare at all.

So, Peace, help me here. Is there something "real" of "real" value waiting to come forth instead of this work that is veneer? Or is the work I've already done "real" work? And do I carry this fear I had not defined in these terms?

All right. Let me give it a try first. I don't think I feel my writing has no value. I think it is as good as much of the writing that is published. But I suppose, then, I would need to ask myself why I have avoided finding a new agent. I'm not sure it was any great subconscious thing at work. First I was busy with work, and at the same time I was giving Dan time to make some response. Then I was busy with the move and the trip. Now I am busy with Christmas. Yet I know that these have not been good enough reasons for someone whose every other thought, as reflected here and elsewhere, concerns my writing. If it were so important to me, so paramount in my life, so integral to my happiness, why didn't I make time for it? I made time for this writing.

Psychologically, I was unprepared for what happened to me, for Dan's quitting agenting. I had thought the need to sell myself was behind me and that I could simply write, and I thought simply writing was what I really wanted to do. But I have not written much other than this. Would I have if things hadn't happened the way they did with Dan? I don't know. I only know that this has been the writing I have wanted to do. I keep saying that I want to get back to my "creative" writing, but the crux of it is that I *don't* want to. There. I have finally admitted it. I am admitting it to myself as I write it. If I had really wanted to get back to it, I would have. If I had really wanted to pursue it, I would have contacted other agents.

This is the writing that has meaning for me now. Whether the writing of mysteries will ever have meaning to me again I do not know. This is what I have been afraid to admit. Because I do want the life of a writer. I do want writing to be my life. And I came so close to making it so with the mystery writing. Will I ever come so close again? Can I really give up something that has for so long held out the promise of giving me the life I want?

What has all my lamenting about my writing really been about? It has been about not knowing what to write while the whole time I have been writing away and finding more solace from it, more wisdom, more peace than I have ever found before. My lamenting has been hanging on for all I am worth to ideas that belonged to the old Margaret, to the Margaret who did not know

299

Peace. Ideas that turned writing into a false god. Ideas that told me all could be achieved through being a published writer instead of that all could be achieved through God. I wanted the life of a writer so I could be proud of myself. I wanted the life of a writer so I would have respect. I wanted the life of a writer so I could share. But what have I been doing? Spending my year taking away all those things that made me feel I could not be proud of myself. Getting rid of all those ideas that said I was not deserving of respect. Sharing.

Even as I write this I am close to tears. Not because of all I have gained, but because of even contemplating giving up what I have thought I have wanted all this time. Grandmother said to give up want. Peace said to give up want. Yet even now, even as I begin to realize how much of what I have wanted I have found, I cannot believe I am even contemplating giving up the goal that has been my goal for so long. It feels like giving up my right arm. It feels like cutting out my heart. It feels like taking my identity away from me. But it also feels like what I must do. I can't even bear to think about it. I don't know what to do.

December 20, 1995

I've got it now. I couldn't hear the message that this message is for the universe because I couldn't bear to give up my fiction. So I asked the Holy Spirit to make my decisions for me after reading in *A Course in Miracles* that He would answer immediately, quietly, with the decision that was right for everyone it touched (which is everyone, not just me). And yesterday, in the midst of my despair, in the midst of my not knowing what to do, Mary Love came to my house, to my table, and told me that what we have lived is the story, our journey is the story, the spirit sisters are the story. She said she had awakened to a message: "This is the story." She came to my table and gave me back my life as writer.

"This is the story." *Our* story—the story of how three ordinary women have shared the journey to oneness—is what I must write. As she told me about it, about how she knew this was what I was meant to do, she went back to her spirit bag and retrieved her journal and read me Trinity's message one more time.

> *As you see you share, all of you do, this unfolds.*
> *The story unfolds. You trust, you share, you grow.*
> *This is life. This is what dreams are made of. This*
> *is LOVE.*

Her voice echoed in my kitchen. Like a shadow on her voice, her words took on added meaning. "This is the story."

I called Julie at work after Mary left and told her what Mary had brought me—told her that we both knew that my next writing was meant to be our story—and asked her if it was all right with her, and if she, too, would participate in the collaboration. She got goose bumps. It's going to be, Peace. I have my answer! I know what I'm supposed to write!

The Holy Spirit, using you and Mary and Trinity as His messengers, has answered me. Mary and Julie and I will collaborate on *our* story. Nothing is stopping me now.

Even one of Gracie's first messages concerned my first book and Christmas. When Mary's computer first started malfunctioning, the file in which Mary had written her note to me concerning her thoughts on *The Ninety-Seven Days* was the only file she was allowed to enter. The cursor went to the word *christmas*, which she had noted as a typo because it was not capitalized, and would not stray from it. It is Christmas. Was Gracie trying to be a messenger too? Was she trying to tell us that by this Christmas we would be working on a book together? Will *our story* be my first book? I do not know but I thank you for this Christmas gift.

December 27, 1995

Peace, I want to thank you for tonight and ask you to help me in keeping this peace. It was my first day back at work since the holidays. Everything went well. I got up and had time before work. I shared the writing I have done on *our story* with the spirit sisters. I did some work. I came home, started salad. Donny came in, made pasta. Angela's boyfriend, Matt, was here. Mia came home from work. We all sat down to dinner together. We laughed like crazy. Donny was at his best lampooning choir and orchestra directors. The kids held their own. They made fun of each other, teased each other, and laughed about it.

After dinner I washed dishes. Mia picked up the table and the pans. Both girls dried while Matt pulled up a chair and strummed his guitar. Donny's nephew, Nick, came in and he and Donny went into Donny's room to play his new Sony system. I came here.

We are all happy, Peace. We are all comfortable. The girls have each other and nice friends and boyfriends. We have our house! We are happy *together.* Thank you to all the powers that be. My life feels as near to perfect as it has ever felt. I have everything I've ever wanted, it seems, and purpose as well.

It is this purpose I want to ask your help with. The writing of this book between the three of us is going to be difficult. Most difficult, probably, for Mary. But also, in a different way, for me. I am used to writing here. I am not used to collaborating. I have left all the garbage stuff behind with the spirit sisters. I know this book couldn't be written while Mary and I still held even the least bit of competitiveness—and luckily we gave that up after Europe. I can't remember right now what, if anything, precipitated the change, but it was there when I returned to work from the trip. I knew, and Mary knew, and Julie knew, and we each knew the other knew, that the old garbage was gone.

This project is not worth bringing it up again. Help me keep it behind me. Help me bring nothing but love here.

Help me stay away particularly from competition, from envy, from comparison. Help me to assure my spirit sisters that they are more important even than the project. Help me stand ready to abandon it in favor of friendship and love if that is what is required. Help me to share my strength with Mary through it if that is what is required.

Peace, Holy Spirit, you started me on this road and I will not fail the right outcome if you stay with me. Don't let me lose you. Don't let my writing ambition rear its ugly head. Let this purpose stay pure, even while I know I don't even realize the extent of my part in this purpose or the extent of this purpose in the world. I want to say, don't let anything mess with my happiness, with my peace; but I know it is my peace that brings me happiness and it is my sharing of my peace that brings much of the happiness to my home and my table.

What a wonderful thing a table is, what treasures we bring there. Please help me to stay in gratitude for my table and its fullness. I am proceeding. I am taking the advice in *A Course in Miracles* literally, and I am not looking back, I am not hesitating or reconsidering. But it wouldn't hurt to feel your reassurance, Peace, your blessing on this course, this purpose. If you have any advice for me on the best way for me to proceed I would love to hear it.

Tell Mary what you just told me. Reassure her. Wait for her to catch up. Take your cues from her. Listen. I believe you. Believe yourself. Your open heart is bringing you wisdom to share. The way is being shown to you. Listen and you will hear.

I will, Peace. I truly am at peace with this project in whatever way it turns out. I know you have told me to proceed and I am at peace with proceeding. But I will be equally at peace with waiting. With giving Mary time. With doing what is needed. I think at my core, at my center, I am truly without ambition in this purpose. It is only at my extremes, on the outer reaches of myself, my old self perhaps, that I worry it will regain ground, that the ego will fool with my peace. That is why I ask your help. Keep my ego out of this project, dear Peace, dear Holy Spirit. Then I know it will proceed as it should proceed, according to God's holy plan.

Thank you for asking, dearest Margaret. Your request has been accomplished.

Dearest Peace   December 31, 1995, New Year's Eve

The year is coming to an end. THE YEAR. Since May 1, I have lived and breathed this year with you. Sometimes I think I have come so far. I have learned so much. And when I do, some old teaching tells me not to praise myself, that it is bad manners. I still have much unlearning to do. And much sharing. But I have come far. So far I am hardly the same person. I am not the person full of shame. I am not the person full of guilt. I am not the person full of resentment. I am not the person full of envy and competition. I am not the slave to time. I am safe. I am beginning. I am new and living in the Now. I feel love almost all the time. I feel gratitude almost all the time. I am often peaceful. I am very often content. I am more into being than searching.

This last has made my communications with you less frequent. This last and love—being with my family and particularly my husband. This last and purpose—working on the goal given me by the Holy Spirit.

Yet I still need your help. I am not full of these negative things anymore. I am happier than I have ever been. I only need a little help, I think, to go the rest of the way. Am I right, Peace? And can you give me the help I need to proceed?

Dearest Margaret,

The year that begins tomorrow will be the first of many years of a new life for you. You do not go into this year or any others unaided. You cannot fail. You cannot go backwards. You carry this Now forward with you. Smell the sweetness of this Now. You are sweet. You are lovely to the heavens. Your happiness brings happiness to the heavens. Let go of illusion. You do it here. You can do it everywhere.

Things are happening for a reason. This you have taught me. Everything happens for a reason, for what it is meant to teach us, bring us. Now today I read in *A Course in Miracles:*

"In any situation in which you are uncertain, the first thing to consider, simply, is 'What do I want to come of this? What is it for?' The clarification of the goal belongs at the beginning, for it is this which will determine the outcome."[25]

I know my reading this today was not an accident. I have seen how you have helped me reach my goals: from my home to my furniture to my car to less stressful periods. Now I know it is time to set a new goal. It is important for the purpose the Holy Spirit has made clear to me, and it is important for this day, this hour, this year—for every situation. For everything that happens that disturbs my peace as well as for everything I want to happen, the question is, "What do I want to come of this? What is it for?"

How seldom we ask these questions! And how difficult to answer. What do I want to come of this? What is it for? I feel it is imperative for us to answer this about *our story,* to set the goal and then have faith. I will work on this with the sisters.

For my own answer, I am uncertain except that I know it is my purpose, given me by the Holy Spirit. Is that goal enough?

That goal is more than enough. That goal is The Goal.

I don't need to define it further?

Do you think the Holy Spirit's goal is to have you embark on this purpose for your own fulfillment alone? Trust that the Holy Spirit sees the grander plan, the picture you would obscure by worrying about the frame. Leave your goal as it is. Do not worry about it. Do not reconsider. Begin. Proceed. Do. Be.

Thank you, Peace.

PEACE

We have been talking at work on how to proceed with writing our story. There has been no lack of permission for me to begin. Mary and I both have journals to draw upon and Julie has an incredible memory. We recently spent an afternoon typing up some of her important dreams and experiences from this year. Her recollection of dates and detail is truly amazing.

It is becoming clear that I will write and that Julie and Mary will guide me, helping me to remember the chain of events that linked our year. Toward this end, I asked Mary if I could read the journal she kept on Grace. I had asked her for it not without tact and gentleness, but with a writer's dispassion. I wanted to see it as a researcher, to know how she felt so that I could bring it to our story.

She had typed it on her computer and printed it out months and months ago. It had been "collecting dust" beneath the bed in the room that would have been Grace's room but which had become Mary's writing room. No one had ever seen this writing.

It has a cover page that says "*Grace's Life* by Mary Kathryn Love." I have now read it.

I seemed to go into another place while I read. I didn't cry, although I felt I should have. But it was as if it emptied me out. It was as if it was so full of feeling, it drained me of feeling, made me numb. But it stayed with me like a vice around my heart. It stayed with me until the moment I returned to work and saw Mary sitting at her desk, a scene I had seen a hundred times, day after day, month after month, and yet, in a way never seen. Mary.

That was when I broke down. I didn't intend to. I didn't know I would. I didn't know something in me had been waiting for the moment of seeing her again. As if I couldn't break down without her. Couldn't shed the tears without sharing them with her. I just hugged her and cried on her shoulder, saying over and over, "Mary, I never knew. I never knew."

I had never known. Never had even the faintest knowing. I thought I had been compassionate. But I had not understood her grief. I had been there. Had thought I had seen. But I had never seen. Some part of me had thought that I could understand her loss in a way that any mother could understand. That I could understand because, as a mother, I could imagine what it would be like to lose a child, because I had almost lost a child. But I hadn't even come close. Now I had. Now I had come close to Mary. Because this writing was Mary.

I told Mary it was the most beautiful writing a mother had ever done about her daughter. It was. It was also the most beautiful writing a woman had ever done about being a mother, about being a woman, about being human and vulnerable. It had everything. The joy of the beginning, the uncertainty, the loss, the ending. It was a tribute to Grace. But it *was* Mary.

It was almost too much. I am not going to be able to be a dispassionate writer, Peace. This is going to ask more from me than I ever imagined. What have I gotten myself into?

I try not to worry about writing the spirit sisters' story. I try to just be in my willingness to proceed. Yet I wonder how to proceed. I worry about time. I worry about energy. I worry about Mary. I worry about the responsibility of it. I worry about my relationship with you.

What is your role now and what is mine? Can I still come to you for answers or is your quietness a sign that the time for this is waning? I am peaceful in comparison to my general state a year ago. I am not peaceful in comparison to my general state a month ago. I feel I know the way now, but not how to get to the starting gate. I hope for the Holy Spirit to illuminate the way and then wonder—again. Peace, I am worried that where I don't get answers, don't get communication, I will get fear. I don't need much to keep me going. I would be happy just to feel you. Mary thinks I have given her some of my peace as I offered her on the phone the other night. I teased today that I felt as if I was having a brain drain.

I worked on our story last night. We're thinking of calling it *Love.* We talked about it at work. I am being very careful with it, not letting fear intrude upon it. It is more "me" that fear is snapping at. Can you help?

I remind you that it is when you are feeling most away from love that I love you most. When fear calls you, ask, "Where is love here?" What has taken you away from feelings of love? It is not me, sweet heart. I am sending you love in abundance. Are you open to receive it?

Have confidence, dear one. We will not let you down. Envision not disaster. Envision not strain and stress. Envision not trauma and uncertainty. Go boldly forward. You are only doubting self. Yet, remember that self is not one. You are not alone. Do not let my quietness or any other thing convince you that you are alone or unworthy of your calling. You have answered The Call. Do you think all of heaven will not rise to answer yours in turn? It will come together. That is what it is all about. Coming together. You are wanting structure before the time for structure. The foundation is taking shape. The structure will follow. Perhaps what you perceive as your weakness will allow others' strengths to emerge.

But you are not weak. There is no weakness, as you perceive weakness, in you. You are very strong. You are not your body. Trust. Trust that the Holy Spirit is doing His job and that He will help you to do yours. Your Peace is with you and you will never lose it by extending it outward. Do not confuse your feelings of weakness and your extension of your peace to Mary. Only know that the answers are being given to you even when they seem not to be the answers. Trust. Have faith. Rest. You have gotten good at extending your love and light. Now practice receiving it. Be a sponge. Drink it in. Feel it. Be grateful for it. Remember the happiness of gratitude and love. Go rest. Feel my love tomorrow. Feel the love of others. You will feel better.

January 5, 1996

In further preparation for writing *Love,* I asked Mary to share her "angel talk" journal writing with me and I have just finished reading it. It is so lovely, so sad, so bitter-sweet, so human, so very human. These fears really are universal, aren't they? And this writing does need to be shared, doesn't it? I read Mary's writing and I think, *How could it fail to move someone, anyone?* No one could be immune.

I realize how little she talks of things that trouble and disappoint her. I can see how when she feels bad, she wills herself not to feel. I understand. I understand her imper-fections and they touch my heart. It is such a knowing. It is such an honor.

And yet, in her writing, she is much as she is in life. Her dramatic way of talking, her sweet way of showing her happiness, her silent way with her sadness. Absolutely nothing there not to love. The innocence of it all. The wanting to be good. To know that the self is lovable. It is hard to fathom that she does not know how lovable she is. How good. How sweet. How kind. How giving.

And I wonder, in retrospect, what my writing sounds like. I am not about to compare myself anymore. But Mary sounds so real. So absolutely true. I thought her writings about Grace were "pure" when I read them, so totally uncontrived, so full of her *self* and all that she was. A pure nakedness of being, feeling, all her pain, love, humanness exposed, vulnerable, pure. What it was. The way you are always saying we *are.* That something *is.* That is what her writing is like.

And I just don't know if I have that pureness in me. And again, I am not saying this in a judgmental way toward myself, only in an acknowledging way, and it is because I am a writer and being a writer is my greatest fear and joy. Can I be uncontrived, can I be just who I am, can I be as pure when I bring all these longings and expectations with me to my writing? I do not know. Perhaps this is my greatest lesson, and how appropriate that I should learn it from Mary. What you have been trying to tell me I needed Mary to learn. I am only realizing this as I write it. The reason I can't fear my writing, can't project, can't bring all the garbage of longing to it is because then it isn't me in all my selfhood; it isn't the essence, the pureness I would like it to be. I realize all writing doesn't have to be all that. And I realize I cannot strive for that. But I also realize I have to drop all the extraneous stuff I bring to my writing.

I hope there has been some pure writing here. I think there has been. But I ask your help, dear Peace, in a way I haven't asked your help in a long time, to bring me back to writing from the heart, and only writing from the heart, because I know that is where truth lies. And I want to bring that heart and that truth to all my writing, but especially to *Love,* Peace. I owe it to Mary and Gracie and Julie and to the heart and truth of the writing Mary shared with me. Will you help me?

You have finally asked the right question. I knew you would. I have been readying everything for this moment. It is done. Rejoice! Let your lingering sadness fall away. It is not only the last barrier with your writing, but also your last barrier with Mary. You would wonder

313

sometimes why your feelings would change from sheer happiness, when you were with her, to nothingness, to feelings of lack. You were no longer competing. You were no longer comparing. But what was it? It was her genuineness, that self that was so purely self, and you wondered, though you did not know it, could not define it, where that genuineness was in you. You have lived with a false front so long, so unknown to self that you became self-conscious. Self-consciousness has today fallen away. Rejoice. You are pure. You are what you Are. Finally, dear Margaret. You can Be. Without pretense.

I assure you that you did not carry pretense here with you often. You never carried it here consciously. Only the longing to overcome it, though you did not know that pretense was what you longed to overcome. Now you can rest. Now you can truly relax with who you are. No need anymore to fool anyone. No need to cover over something unworthy with a veneer of goodness. Your goodness is genuine, dear one. It was only the veneer that tarnished it. Rejoice that you do not need it anymore. It is over now. You can truly rest. You can find joy now. No more need to polish the silver. You are gold! Nothing to work on anymore. It is done. All you have to do is BE. The work has all been in the polishing what was already a jewel you only thought was coal. Go and be the jewel you are. But first get the rest, the first real rest, the rest of the completed, the one, the finished, the united. The work is done. Rest.

Dearest Peace,   January 6, 1996

When I finished here last night, I went up and wrote in my dream journal about how important your last message and the moments with you here were to me. How grateful I am. I did rest well. I didn't wake up fully until

11:30 this morning. I have had a lovely day cleaning and puttering and putting away the Christmas decorations. Preparing, finally, for the New Year and all its possibilities. I am just so grateful, Peace, for everything. I love my home so much I even love cleaning it. I love just being with my family. I would like it to go on forever—it is heaven to me, right here, right now. And I know this is where you have wanted me to be all along. Thank you for getting me here, Peace, and for all the help you've given me and sent me on the way.

I wanted to call Mary and be with her and share what had come to me from her writing. Do you realize, Peace—of course you do!—that she even had a dream the night before last about trying to solve a mystery and the mystery concerned me finding someone? It was me, wasn't it, Peace? The *me* hidden behind the veneer. Not just the writing—as in my dream—but *me!* I was lost and now I am found. I AM FOUND!

I went to sleep last night, Peace, repeating to myself, "I am who I am, I need do nothing. The work is done. I can rest." It was so sweet, Peace. Such a gentle place. I think I may even have relaxed.

I've been typing the rest of Mary's journal. This is the one she kept when she was unable to get into the computer to write. I thought by typing it, it would be available for use in *Love* and it would also really get it into my head. I was right. I was only going to type sections. Only those things I thought might be useful. But I cannot exclude

315

anything. I'm continuing to type not so much for *Love* as for a gift for Mary. And perhaps for me. I am still with her today even though I did not call her and we did not get together. I know it is a weekend when her stepdaughter, Amanda, is with her and I did not want to intrude.

My body is getting tired of typing, and yet I want to finish. I will break in a little while until tomorrow—don't think I'll finish tonight—and I know it's not important to. I can wake up to Mary again tomorrow. Peace, I have been hoping there would be a Christmas miracle and Mary would get pregnant. She desires it so greatly. It is to her what my writing is to me—her greatest desire and her greatest fear. If my prayers are being heard, Oh Lord, let this happen for Mary. Bring her this joy. I hope we are both now open to having our dreams fulfilled. I feel in my heart you have brought us to this place—together. It would be such a sweet bond, to seal our growth with the happiness of our heart's desire. If it is Your Will.

Peace, I have no questions for you tonight. No pains. No frustrations. I bring you only my gratitude and my greetings. Do you have greetings for me, dear friend, best friend, friend of my heart and soul?

What a lovely greeting, dear one. Your happiness is assured. Happiness is enjoying the Now. As long as you remember what you have felt and seen the last few days, you will be happy. You will know your heart's desire as you have never known it before and it will be. You no longer need anything to make you happy. You need nothing and you need do nothing. Do not begin again to strive and plan. You know your immedi-

ate purpose. You are preparing for it with love. You will complete it with love. No striving or planning are required. LET IT BE.

I must say thank you, also, for the music of the Beatles. You know I thought of their song "Let It Be" last night in connection to Mary. I don't know if they are guides or their music tools for you, my guides, but I thank you for it. I am just so grateful for everything. I cannot tell you enough, thank you enough. Any parting words, my friend?

The world, the universe is your friend tonight, dear one. All is friendship and love. All is right with the world. Your corner of it is expanding. The beauty of your home is yours to keep and to share. Trust that what will make you happy will come to you even if it is not what you thought it would be. Think of your striving for happiness this way— think of all the "things" you have striven for in the past. Did you know then what would make you happy? If you strive for red shoes, you may not find the blue that will make your feet dance. Just LET IT BE. And rest. Leave it all to me and the Holy Spirit. We know God's plan. God's plan includes more happiness for you than you can imagine. LET IT BE. And we will take you there.

Thank you, dear Friend, dear Guide, dear Messenger of the Divine. All my love, Margaret.

EPIPHANY

Dearest Peace,   January 7, 1996
    I went to church this morning. It reminds me
of how I began this writing. With a trip to church,
with the residual awareness that comes from that hour of
contemplation and ritual.

Today we were celebrating Jesus' baptism and the feast
of the Epiphany. The moment Jesus was identified as *who
He was.* Again my life is mirroring my faith, my religion,
my God, and the calendar year. I looked up *epiphany* in the
dictionary today while Mary was here with me, sharing
with me the wonderful occurrences of the last two

days—my identity, my becoming *who I am.* Here is what we found together, with the accompanying goose bumps, of course:

> epiphany: from the Greek *epiphaneia,* appearance, to show forth, manifest
> 1. an appearance or manifestation of a god or other supernatural being
> 2. in many Christian churches, a yearly festival, held January 6, commemorating both the revealing of Jesus as the Christ to the Gentiles in the persons of the Magi and the baptism of Jesus: also called twelfth day [Mary told me as in the twelve days of Christmas.]
> 3. (a) a moment of sudden intuitive understanding; flash of insight (b) a scene, experience, etc., that occasions such a moment

Peace, I had my Epiphany! With the church's Epiphany! With Jesus! and with Mary and you. I had it here, I had it inside. I am identified. I am without my veneer, my covering over. I am Me.

I can only say thank you again. I am grateful again. All over again. Fresh today. Freshly grateful. Freshly *Who I Am.*

It was a blessing to be able to share it with Mary, who

gave me the gift of *Who She Is* so that I might have this gift of *Who I Am.* And although Julie wasn't with us, there was another part of it, Peace, a part that pulls her in (because of her angel being Water and water being such an important symbol for her). Today was also the day that holy water is blessed. The holy water of baptism: of rebirth. I got holy water for Julie and Mary and will give it to both of them tomorrow.

> baptism: from the Latin Christian baptism, a dipping under
> 1. a baptizing or being baptized; specif. the ceremony or sacrament of admitting a person into Christianity or a specific Christian church by immersing the individual in water or by pouring or sprinkling water on the individual, as a symbol of washing away sin and of spiritual purification
> 2. any experience or ordeal that initiates, tests, or purifies

Oh, Peace. It purifies! Of course. And that is the gift you and Mary and God have given me: the gift of being newly purified—not only my writing—but me.

Is there anything further I need do to purify my union with Julie? Something still seems to stand between us at times. Was it only my veneer or is there something else?

Can you guide me, either here or when next I see her, as to how to leave the barriers behind?

The barriers are gone from you. Do not even remember them. See Julie only with your open heart and give her space in which to open to you. She is still just a little bit afraid. Seeing what Knowing each other has done for you and Mary will help her. This helping each other and giving gifts to each other is what it is all about. Be gentle with her while she unwraps her gift. I assure you when the gift is opened, it will be one of love, and the bonding, the transformation, will be complete.

THIS IS THE STORY. This unfolding. It is not over. The work is done but the story continues. For a lifetime. This is how destiny is revealed. How the talent, the uniqueness, the special gifts of each are brought to the open. Are given space to be. This is only the beginning. A lifetime of happiness awaits. Do not delay. The time has come. You are in it. The time is Now.

Thank you, sweet Peace. I will not delay. I am IN IT.

EPILOGUE

When this work was first being considered for publication, it was suggested that the passages concerning my desire to become a published writer would need to be deleted. "Writers don't talk about writing unless they are writing a book on writing," I was told. I think this mandate also had to do with the uncomfortableness of my publisher, Dan Odegard, in being included in the content of a book he would publish.

But after the more careful consideration of my editor, Steve Lehman, it was decided that my desire had to be included. Because what we desire is at the center of our lives—is our own central theme when we are considering who we are. If everywhere that I talked about my writing you inserted your own desire, you may have learned a lesson similar to the one I learned. Whether we desire power or wealth, talent or the recognition of talent, children or grandchildren, the perfect relationship or the perfect occupation, what we desire is the grand determiner of how we see ourselves in relation to the world around us. It can be the key that unlocks all the rest or the locked door that bars our entrance to everything beyond it.

My journey with Peace was one of taking my desire and identifying its true nature. Of finding the truth within my desire. My original desire to write was not about this writing. The choice to share this writing was a difficult but necessary one. That choice being to be who I am. Because by the time I had finished *Peace,* I was no longer a mystery writer. My desire no longer had to do with writing mysteries.

The decision to share this writing was a difficult one because I was afraid of admitting I was talking to an angel, afraid of admitting I had chosen a spiritual life, afraid to change the image of myself as "mystery writer" that I had held on to for so long. I was not afraid to write mystery novels that dealt with tortured souls and the darkest hours of life. But I was afraid to write about the real mystery of discovering that there was something beyond myself that could help me bring my own tortured soul to the light.

Dan Odegard was the mysterious "link" between the person I thought I was when I began my journey and the person I have since become. The link that eventually brought the Peace writing to the light. When Dan was my agent, I looked to him, especially in the early days of my spiritual quest, as being as much an answer to my prayers as Peace later became. He was going to be the "agent" who provided me with the means for doing what I wanted to do with my life: write. And I quite simply had faith in his ability to do so.

But then the day came when I received his letter saying that he was leaving the agenting profession for a position in publishing at Hazelden. The letter came two days after I had begun visualizing his finding me a publisher. The letter came on the very day on which my astrologer, Pat, had predicted I would have a publisher.

I thought Dan's leaving the agenting profession was terrible news. I did not, of course, know then that Hazelden would become the publisher of *The Grace Trilogy* or even that *The Grace Trilogy* would be written. I still thought of myself then as a mystery writer.

But for some reason, despite the "bad" news, I continued to have faith in Dan. I continued to believe, as I told Peace, that, "He would be my bridge to the publishing world." He was.

Was this a small miracle? A divine coincidence? I prefer to think of it as the natural outcome of faith. There were many more divine coincidences that led to the publication of *The Grace Trilogy*. It was as if some unseen force was moving around the puzzle pieces of many lives, bringing them together to make this work available to you. I have no doubt, any longer, of what that unseen force was.

This is the final message I leave you with. What we have faith in becomes an agent to bring us what we truly desire. What we truly desire, when given to God, brings God to us. Because what we desire was given to us by God to bring us to Him.

Peace.

NOTES

1. James Hillman, *Insearch: Psychology and Religion* (Woodstock, Conn.: Spring Publishers, 1994), 40.

2. Hillman, *Insearch*, 50.

3. Hillman, *Insearch*, 56.

4. Hillman, *Insearch*, 65.

5. Joan Borysenko, *Fire in the Soul: A New Psychology of Spiritual Optimism* (New York: Warner Books, 1993), 154–57.

6. Thomas Moore, *Soul Mates: Honoring the Mysteries of Love and Relationship* (New York: HarperCollins, 1994), 94–95.

7. Borysenko, *Fire in the Soul*, 154.

8. Borysenko, *Fire in the Soul*, 154–55.

9. Borysenko, *Fire in the Soul*, 156–57.

10. Rollo May, *Freedom and Destiny* (New York: Bantam Doubleday Dell, 1981), 241–42.

11. Aldous Huxley, *The Perennial Philosophy* (New York: Harper Colophon, 1970), 125.

12. Huxley, *The Perennial Philosophy*, 131.

13. Pat Rodegast and Judith Stanton, *Emmanuel's Book III: What Is an Angel Doing Here?* (New York: Bantam, 1994), 237.

14. Duane Elgin, *Voluntary Simplicity: Toward a Way of Life That Is Outwardly Simple, Inwardly Rich* (New York: Morrow Quill Paperbacks, 1981), 137.

15. John Spayde, quoted in *Utne Reader* (Jan–Feb 1995): no. 67, 56.

16. David Jay Brown and Rebecca McClen Novick, ed., excerpts from an interview with Carolyn Mary Kleefeld in *Mavericks of the Mind: Conversations for the New Millennium* (Freedom, Calif.: The Crossing Press, 1993), 157–72.

17. Brown and Novick, *Mavericks of the Mind*, 167.

18. Sogyal Rinpoche, *The Tibetan Book of Living and Dying* (New York: HarperCollins Publishers, 1992), 102–3.

19. Larry Dossey. *Healing Words: The Power of Prayer and the Practice of Medicine* (New York: HarperCollins Publishers, 1993), 22.

20. Rev. Hugo Hoever, ed., *Lives of the Saints* (New York: Catholic Book Publishing, 1955), 386, 387.

21. Willis Harman and Howard Rheingold, *Higher Creativity: Liberating the Unconscious for Breakthrough Insights* (Los Angeles: Tarcher, 1984), 226.

22. Hillman, *Insearch*, 40.

23. James A. Swan, ed., *The Power of Place: Sacred Ground in Natural and Human Environments* (Wheaton, Ill.: Quest Books, The Theosophical Publishing House, 1991), 324.

24. Swan, *The Power of Place*, 333.

25. *A Course in Miracles* (Mill Valley, Calif.: Foundation for Inner Peace, 1993), 366.

ABOUT THE AUTHOR

Margaret Perron majored in English at the University of Minnesota where she won the Jean Keller-Bouvier Award for literary accomplishment. She has been a public relations director in the nonprofit sector and has worked in administration at the University of Minnesota while pursuing her interest in writing. She grew up in St. Paul, Minnesota, where she continues to find sustenance from her faith, her friends, and her family. Perron is currently a Program Associate for the ISP Executive Study Program at the University of Minnesota. She can be contacted through the web site of The Grace Foundation: http://www.gracezurilovefoundation.com

Hazelden Publishing and Education is a division of the Hazelden Foundation, a not-for-profit organization. Since 1949, Hazelden has been a leader in promoting the dignity and treatment of people afflicted with the disease of chemical dependency.

The mission of the foundation is to improve the quality of life for individuals, families, and communities by providing a national continuum of information, education, and recovery services that are widely accessible; to advance the field through research and training; and to improve our quality and effectiveness through continuous improvement and innovation.

Stemming from that, the mission of the publishing division is to provide quality information and support to people wherever they may be in their personal journey—from education and early intervention, through treatment and recovery, to personal and spiritual growth.

Although our treatment programs do not necessarily use everything Hazelden publishes, our bibliotherapeutic materials support our mission and the Twelve Step philosophy upon which it is based. We encourage your comments and feedback.

The headquarters of the Hazelden Foundation are in Center City, Minnesota. Additional treatment facilities are located in Chicago, Illinois; New York, New York; Plymouth, Minnesota; St. Paul, Minnesota; and West Palm Beach, Florida. At these sites, we provide a continuum of care for men and women of all ages. Our Plymouth facility is designed specifically for youth and families.

For more information on Hazelden, please call **1-800-257-7800.** Or you may access our World Wide Web site on the Internet at **http://www.hazelden.org**.